THE REAL READER

Slightly Foxed

'Manhattan Moments'

NO.59   AUTUMN 2018

Editors Gail Pirkis & Hazel Wood
Marketing & publicity Stephanie Allen & Jennie Harrison Bunning
Bookshops Anna Kirk
Subscriptions Hattie Summers & Olivia Wilson

Cover illustration: Luna North, 'Beechnuts'
Luna North trained at the Falmouth School of Art. She now lives in Devon where she specializes in printmaking. The images in her linocuts of native flora and fauna are inspired by the wild landscape around her and are designed and carved in the Romantic tradition. Her work can be seen in galleries throughout the UK and has recently been exhibited in New York. More examples, and contact details, can be found on her website www.lunanorth.co.uk.

Design by Octavius Murray

Layout by Andrew Evans

Colophon and tailpiece by David Eccles

© The contributors 2018

Published by Slightly Foxed Limited
53 Hoxton Square
London N1 6PB

tel 020 7033 0258
email office@foxedquarterly.com
www.foxedquarterly.com

Slightly Foxed is published quarterly in early March, June, September and December

Annual subscription rates (4 issues)
UK and Ireland £40; Overseas £48

Single copies of this issue can be bought for £11 (UK) or £13 (Overseas)

All back issues in printed form are also available

ISBN 978-1-910898-21-5
ISSN 1742-5794

Printed and bound by Smith Settle, Yeadon, West Yorkshire

Contents

Contents

John Watson

For the digital edition of *Slightly Foxed* and an up-to-date list of partners
and membership benefits, please visit the members' page on our website:
www.foxedquarterly.com/members or contact Olivia:
olivia@foxedquarterly.com · +44 (0) 20 7033 0258

The Slightly Foxed office can obtain all books reviewed in this issue,
whether new or second-hand. Please contact Anna:
anna@foxedquarterly.com · +44 (0) 20 7033 0258

From the Editors

'For weeks the trees had been heavy-laden with tired green leaves,' writes BB when autumn arrives in *Brendon Chase*, 'but now! What glory! What a colour ran riot in the underwood, how sweet and keen became the morning air.' This is the season when 'a new zest for living stirs within the blood, [and] adventure beckons in every yellowing leaf'. And sure enough, here at Hoxton Square, we're in a decidedly adventurous mood.

Some adventures span whole careers and have an endearingly absurd character at their heart. So it is with Jennie Erdal's wickedly funny *Ghosting: A Double Life*, the latest of our Slightly Foxed Editions (see p. 14). Erdal spent twenty years ghost-writing for 'Tiger', a flamboyant independent publisher who was determined to write books as well as publish them – despite limited literary talent. She created a whole oeuvre in Tiger's name, even turning his ludicrous plot ideas and sexual fantasies into novels which were seriously and admiringly reviewed. *Ghosting* is her brilliant memoir of that time, colourful in its treatment of Tiger's wild enthusiasms and weird obsessions but also subtle and multi-layered, as Erdal explores the emotional dissonance that comes from living life behind a mask, pretending to feel one thing when experiencing another.

There are wild enthusiasms of a very different sort in BB's *Brendon Chase* (see p. 31), the third book by this exceptionally gifted children's writer to be reissued in our Slightly Foxed Cubs series. In it, we follow three brothers as they escape from their aunt's house one night at the end of the Easter holidays, fleeing the prospect of school and living instead in a hollow oak tree in the middle of an eleven-thousand-acre forest. There are gripping adventures and plenty of high jinks as the boys narrowly evade capture – and there are moments of quiet reverie too, as we tread the forest paths with the boys in search of birds' nests, butterflies and the Blind Pool. This is a book for readers young and not so young – for anyone, in fact, who knows the delights of days spent wandering in the woods, well out of reach of the grown-ups.

If one can't escape to an oak tree in these uncertain times, one can at least find refuge in life's humour and absurdity. And for that, we have Dr Philip Evans who, each Christmas for the past sixteen years, has sent his friends and family a small booklet of 'wonders and absurdities' gleaned from many different sources over the year. When he sent the booklets to us they made us laugh so much we decided to publish a selection. The result is *A Country Doctor's Commonplace Book*, a very individual look at the eccentricities of English life from a well-read man with a keen sense of humour. Of all his sources, among our favourites are announcements from the newsletter of the Lark Valley Benefice ('The sermon topic tonight will be "What is Hell?" Come early and listen to our choir practice'). The ideal gift to cheer a friend or slip into a dear one's Christmas stocking.

And finally, we have a rather exciting announcement of our own: we are nearly ready to launch the Slightly Foxed Podcast. Think of it as an audio version of *Slightly Foxed*, full of interesting bookishness, interviews and discussion – all set around our kitchen table, here in Hoxton Square. We hope it will be the sort of book programme we'd want to listen to ourselves, and we'll be letting you know more about it nearer the time. Adventurous indeed!

GAIL PIRKIS & HAZEL WOOD

Manhattan Moments

KRISTIAN DOYLE

In January 1954, a vignette appeared in the *New Yorker*'s 'Talk of the Town' section, introduced only vaguely as a missive from 'a rather long-winded lady'. The piece – like all 'Talk' stories then, unsigned – was a lightly sardonic first-person account of a woman's disastrous experience in a dress shop. It might not have been world-changing, but it did stand out from the usual 'Talk' pieces, which were often impersonal, mannered little things, written in the royal 'we'. The Long-Winded Lady, though, idiosyncratic from the beginning, spoke only for herself. 'Well, there you are,' she signed off, 'in case you've paid any attention.'

Such pieces, ostensibly slight essays on life in Manhattan, continued to appear, on and off, until 1981. They were always unsigned, and introduced only with a phrase like 'Our friend the long-winded lady has written to us as follows', but when in 1969 a collection was assembled for publication, the writer's identity was revealed. She was, it turned out, Maeve Brennan, an Irish author of short stories and a *New Yorker* staff writer.

This revelation was a shame, I reckon. It's hard now to take these odd little pieces – quasi-anonymous, after all – in the manner in which they were intended. Brennan's life – which in tabloid-headline form runs something like 'ultra-elegant model for Holly Golightly

Maeve Brennan, *The Long-Winded Lady: Notes from the New Yorker* (1998)
Stinging Fly Press · Pb · 222pp · £10.99 · ISBN 9781906539597

ends up mad bag lady' – casts a long shadow over her work, particularly this side of the Atlantic, where none of her books was published in her lifetime. It's arguable, in fact, that the subsequent biography of her, as much as the work itself, was responsible for the mini-revival she underwent at the turn of the millennium. You can see why. 'Mad, destitute writer' makes good copy. Add to that the *Breakfast at Tiffany's* glamour, and the tragic-downfall articles write themselves.

I was lucky to come across the essays when I was too young to know about the *New Yorker*, never mind Maeve Brennan. To me, they were just prose snapshots of city life taken by an archetype with which – having been raised in a busy city myself – I was familiar: the quietly eccentric urban solitary. And that first impression lingers. I see her in every city I visit.

In the earliest pieces, the Long-Winded Lady is a two-dimensional comedic persona, that of a well-heeled suburbanite shopping her way around the nicer parts of Manhattan. But as the essays keep coming, the character deepens. A noticeable change occurs in 1960, when Brennan, aged 43, goes through a divorce and, after time spent away, returns to the city alone. The humour turns brittle, and melancholy, hitherto repressed, starts to predominate. The Long-Winded Lady from this point comes very close indeed to reflecting her writer's character and its vicissitudes.

Keeping to her parts of Manhattan – Midtown and Greenwich Village mainly – the Long-Winded Lady eavesdrops on 'the most cumbersome, most reckless, most ambitious, most confused, most comical, the saddest and coldest and most human of cities', as Brennan calls it in her note to the 1969 collection. Sometimes she watches the world from her window or, if her current room has one (she moves *a lot*), her balcony. Mostly she's out, though, ambling through the most vital, open streets in the world. She hears that a wooden farmhouse is being transported from Uptown to Greenwich Village and goes to see it ('Charles Street is a nice street, a good place for a house to move to'). She visits the local haberdashery to inspect the damage from a fire whose smoke she saw the night before. She watches a parade, or a protest. She shops for shoes or books or, once, 'one of those plain glass orange squeezers'. Her favourite activity, though, is watching the goings-on in 'small, inexpensive restaurants', which she believes are 'the home fires of New York City'.

'It is not the strange or exotic ways of people that interest her,' Brennan writes in the same note, 'but the ordinary ways, when something that is familiar to her shows.' Her style is built upon this ordinariness, and it's one of the reasons she was referred to – when referred to at all – as Chekhovian. Her metaphors, like his, manage to be both rich and remarkably close to their occasion: a man enters a restaurant with a bundle of newspapers 'which had been opened and folded back carelessly so they looked half inflated and as though they might start to rise, like a soufflé, at any minute'. Chekhovian too is the way she matter-of-factly deals with the peculiarities of ordinary perception, as when describing the view from a restaurant window that's partly below street level: 'you see . . . halves of men and women, whole children, and dogs complete from nose to tip of tail'. Where she differs from Chekhov, though, is in her inevitable return to introspection. This is how that observation ends: 'It is both soothing and interesting to watch people without being able to see their faces. It is like counting sheep.' This is less like Chekhov and more like a character in Chekhov. That's the better way to think about it: the Long-Winded Lady pieces are not so much stories as soliloquies. Hers is the only consciousness we really inhabit.

That isn't to say her world is full of stick figures, though. People are merely observed and briefly noted, yet how vivid they are. In the phrase used by Ford Madox Ford, they are quickly 'got in'. Ford, to illustrate this point, uses a Maupassant sentence: 'He was a gentleman with red whiskers who always went first through a doorway.' 'That gentleman', Ford writes, 'is so sufficiently got in that you need no more of him to understand how he will act.' The same could be said of many of the Long-Winded Lady's characters. Take for example 'The Man Who Combs His Hair' (1964): 'There is a man around this neighbourhood who is always combing his hair. Once I saw him borrow a comb from a very small shoeshine boy. Then, while he combed his hair, combing it with one hand and smoothing it with the other, he bent and looked into the child's face as though the little face were a mirror – only a mirror, and nothing more than that.'

Her sensitivity to people, and her ability to vivify them with only a brief sketch, must have had something to do with my delay in grasping one of the essential – and terrifying – facts about the Long-Winded Lady: *she is only ever alone.* No matter how many fellow New Yorkers she observes, she's never actually with any of them. She dines alone, drinks alone, shops alone, walks alone, lives alone. She talks only to the odd stranger (almost always reluctantly), and shop, hotel, bar and restaurant staff. Even in a piece about a New Year's Eve gathering – fourteen of whose attendees she names and evidently knows well – she seems apart, an observer watching alone.

It's hard to think of anyone other than maybe Rilke or Pessoa whose work this sort of loneliness pervades so strongly. And yet this is someone at the very centre of cosmopolitan society: a *New Yorker* staff writer who has romances with some of the magazine's biggest names and is friends with Capote, Gerald and Sara Murphy (on whom Fitzgerald based the Divers of *Tender Is the Night*), Edward Albee . . .

Her friend Roger Angell's verdict – 'She wasn't one of us; she was one of her' – approaches it. It's not so much a physical as an inner apartness – one that, usually, she's comfortable with. Look at the Long-Winded Lady's peculiar attitude towards seeing celebrities on the streets: 'I like recognizing them . . . and knowing that by just being where I am they make me invisible.' That apartness is also there, though less comfortably, in her occasional bitterness when describing groups or couples enjoying themselves. Of a woman strolling with her boyfriend, she writes: 'Her hair had been bleached and dyed so often that it was weathered to a rough rust-pink, and it hung stiffly down her back like a mane, or like wig hair before it has been brushed and combed and curled into shape.' She goes on: the couple 'were the same height (five feet four or so) and about the same weight (a hundred and sixty pounds)'. There's something fearful about such a cruel eye. It makes the beholder herself seem fragile and exposed.

The Long-Winded Lady reserves her sympathy almost exclusively for animals, trees and those lower in society. 'I like pigeons,' she writes. 'I cannot imagine where they get their pampered air, but they have it and I like them for having it.' She gives 'a cheer for the cleaning lady' who, telling the press of coming across a bag of jewels, said, 'My eyes popped out . . . I couldn't resist first trying on a few rings and bracelets.' And when beggars ask her for money, she gives it.

She's also gentle (though slightly mocking in a collegial way) with fellow solitaries. She admires, for example, a woman she encounters while shopping, who hums while she browses: 'Every time she saw something that interested her, her humming rose a little, and by the time she went off to the fitting room, with several dresses, she had almost achieved a soft chant of triumph.'

Towards the city itself – which, directly or indirectly, is her work's focus – the Long-Winded Lady is fiercely ambivalent. It's clear that she loves it. Yet she seems to love it against her will – particularly in her middle and later years, when Manhattan was the chaotic site of one of the biggest building booms in history. Midtown especially suffered at the hands of so-called urban renewal: whole areas were demolished to make way for skyscrapers – areas Brennan knew well, and had often lived in. As early as 1955 the Long-Winded Lady was prophesying (correctly): 'All my life, I suppose, I'll be scurrying out of buildings just ahead of the wreckers.'

She saw first hand that such vandalism was the death of many New York neighbourhoods. Though far from perfect, these were self-sustaining, integrated communities, in which people walked to work, watched their streets, knew one another – places whose small businesses were run by the locals who owned them. Their destruction, combined with city-wide problems such as financial turmoil, the departure of industry and the middle classes, and a drug epidemic, also led to a rapid rise in crime. Between 1959 and 1971 (the bulk of her career), killings in New York more than quadrupled.

You can see the decline by looking at the films from that period. The harshly glamorous Times Square of *The Sweet Smell of Success* (1957) becomes, in just over a decade, the crime-ridden sleaze-pit of *Midnight Cowboy* (1969). By the time you get to *Taxi Driver* in 1976, Manhattan is close to its nadir. This isn't just cinematic over-statement, either. In 1975, the city was at its lowest point since the Depression, almost going bankrupt. It wasn't until 1981, the year of the Long-Winded Lady's final letter, that it finally balanced the books and began to revive.

'These days I think of New York as the capsized city,' Brennan writes in the 1969 note. 'Half-capsized, anyway, with the inhabitants hanging on, most of them still able to laugh as they cling to the island that is their life's predicament.' She herself was one such inhab-itant – though, in the later pieces at least, she's seldom laughing. The artful reticence and gentle mockery of the Long-Winded Lady's early stories make way for full-throated despair, as in one of her most revealing pieces, 'I Look Down from the Windows of This Old Broadway Hotel' (1967). This is the centre of New York's theatrical and entertainment area, she writes,

> but what joviality and good fellowship exist here are thin; the atmosphere is of shabby transience, and its heart is inimical. It is a run-down neighbourhood of cheap hotels and rooming houses and offices and agencies and studios and restaurants and bars, and of shops that pack up and disappear overnight . . . The blank windows reflect an extremity of loneliness – that mechanical city loneliness which strays always at the edge of chaos, far from sol-itude . . . Ordinary life used to be lived [here] . . . but it has come to be hardly more than a camping ground for strollers and trav-ellers and tourists and transients of every kind.

'A few people stay,' she goes on, and in a sad reverie she imagines one: 'an old woman living by herself in a single hotel bedroom' who, suddenly fearful but without anyone to talk to, 'tries to tell the room clerk of what is threatening her'. He listens, 'but he has heard her story many times before, from other people, in other years and in other defeated places like this one'. In the light of Brennan's own future – alone, poor, paranoid, drifting from one seedy single hotel room to another on nearby 42nd Street (which the *New York Times* once called 'the worst block in town') – it's upsettingly prescient. But, fortunately, the Long-Winded Lady's long-windedness offers something else on which to close. It might be my favourite of her endings, managing to be somehow both dreamlike and grounded, and with that characteristic note, in its final line, of faint, faint hope.

'I heard', she writes, 'the music of a very small band – and the tune being played was small and sweet and noticeably free: elfin music.' (That odd adjective was often used to describe Brennan herself.) Then 'a man came into view . . . He was the band.' After describing, minutely, this one-man band's equipment, she writes, 'He banged the drum and blew the trumpet and clashed the cymbals and piped on a little pipe, but although the street was fairly busy, nobody gave him any attention . . .' Suddenly, a car, racing into the nearby car-park, brushes him. 'I got a fright,' writes the Long-Winded Lady,

> but the musician showed no sign of fright, or anxiety, or anger – not a sign of interest. He continued banging the drum, clashing the cymbal, blowing the trumpet; his music never faltered. Imperturbable, he advanced along his way and passed out of my sight behind the little houses just below me . . . I thought he might turn around and come back to Broadway this way, but he did not come back – at least, not while I waited.

KRISTIAN DOYLE is a writer who lives in Liverpool. He is currently at work on a novel.

Tiger the Literary Lion

HAZEL WOOD

One day in 1981 a young woman found herself travelling from her Scottish home to London to meet a publisher. So far so predictable perhaps. She had read Russian at university and had recently translated the memoirs of the painter Leonid Pasternak, father of the more famous Boris. There was nothing predictable about this meeting, however, and the man waiting for her at the door of his Mayfair flat was no ordinary publisher. This is how she describes him.

> So strange and exotic is he that he could be a rare tropical bird that you might never come face to face with, even in a lifetime spent in the rain forest. The plumage is a wonder to behold: a large sapphire in the lapel of a bold striped suit, a vivid silk tie so bright that it dazzles, and when he flaps his wings the lining of his jacket glints and glistens like a prism. He takes my hand and lays it on the silk lining. *You want to touch? Go on, touch! It's best Chinese silk. I have only the best.*

Over the next twenty years, she and 'Tiger', as she calls this unnamed (but easily identifiable) publisher, would become inextricably intertwined. He would become her financial saviour and she would become his voice, expressing on paper the fantasies he was unable to express for himself, massaging his ego and turning him into the literary lion he longed to be. This is the story she tells in *Ghosting*. For a while I inhabited the strange, liminal world of the ghost-writer myself and a friend gave a copy to me as a present when it was first published in 2004. I thought it one of the cleverest, most original and entertaining memoirs I'd ever read. Reading it again years later I still do.

It all started like this. Leonid Pasternak had done paintings of Tiger's Palestinian homeland and Tiger was desperate to buy them. When he made contact with Jennie Erdal, translator of the painter's memoirs, she told him she knew they were not for sale, but Tiger persuaded her to accompany him on this apparently hopeless mission. In Oxford, he was confronted by Pasternak's high-minded daughter Josephine, determined not to sell. Tiger went to work:

> In the presence of the publisher's fine plumage and splendid colours, this sensible woman became girlish and coquettish . . . He eulogised the artist, he emoted over the lost land of Palestine, he flattered and fawned, buttered and oiled. It was a spectacular show, fascinating to watch. After a feeble fight Josephine Pasternak succumbed to the seductive display. She sold him the paintings.

It was Erdal's first experience of Tiger's formidable powers of persuasion. Before she left that day he had also signed her up as a commissioning editor in charge of a new Russian list. It seemed a perfect arrangement. She could work from home – she was married with three young children – making only occasional forays to London to meet Tiger and attend meetings.

What she saw when she did astonished her. These were the colourful days of independent publishing, before the grey suits and conglomerates took over. Tiger's was a small firm with a bold reputation, run entirely according to its owner's likes and dislikes. Surrounding him was a harem of beautiful, well-connected girls, Cosimas, Selinas, Lucindas, Candidas, all employed in vague capacities and competing for his attention while pursuing their own busy social lives. Their presence seemed to dominate the office. Expensive changes of clothing hung in doorways and over the backs of chairs, telephones rang, kettles boiled, hairdryers hummed, and there was 'a lot of shrieking and embracing'.

Tiger adored the attention. 'Do you like my girls?' he asked Erdal.

'They are amazing, isn't it?' To Erdal, with her austere Scottish upbringing, this world was strange and bewildering. But, while observing it all with a cool, appraising eye, she buckled down and taught herself to edit.

This arrangement might have continued indefinitely but for a sudden turn of events. Her husband announced he had fallen in love with someone else and would be leaving. She was devastated. Eventually she told Tiger, who reacted with kindness and concern and next day phoned with a proposition. He had had a 'brilliant idea': a book that would be 'unprecedented' in the world of publishing. He would conduct a series of interviews with high-profile women: Erdal's job would be to devise interview questions, edit the results and put the volume together. 'This book will be *sensational*,' said Tiger. 'I guarantee it.' She would make some money and, he said, it would take her mind off things.

What could she do but agree? It was the thin end of the wedge. Amazingly, warmed by the sun of Tiger's attention, women as serious as Doris Lessing began to spill the beans. He was over the moon. The original target of twenty-five interviews increased to a hundred, then two, then three. He was so excited he couldn't stop. Meantime, up in Fife, Erdal, with the help of co-opted friends, was labouring literally day and night to edit the transcripts and get the work done in time for that year's Frankfurt Book Fair, with Tiger constantly, melodramatically, disturbingly on the phone, transmitting a high level of anxiety.

The book, when published, was of biblical proportions, but it was surprisingly well-received. Tiger's interview with the French politician Edith Cresson, in which she claimed that one in four Anglo-Saxon men was gay, even gave rise to a question in Parliament. Foreign rights were sold and Tiger was ecstatic. Erdal was grateful for the money, but the unrelenting work had taken its toll: within months she was in hospital with severe psoriasis. At the same time her house was threatened with repossession. Again Tiger came to the rescue, loaning her enough money to buy out her husband and secure the children's home.

By now Tiger was not merely a publisher but something of a literary figure, regularly commissioned by newspapers to write articles and reviews – all of them in fact written by Erdal. Sometimes they travelled together to Tiger's plush retreat in the Dordogne, France being 'the best place in the world to create'. She did the creating while he did the phoning to London with progress reports on his creativity. It was on one of these trips that he broke the bad news. He wanted to write a novel. It was to be a love story.

'What sort of love story do we have in mind?' I ask, as if we are discussing wallpaper or home furnishing and he has to pick one from a limited range. 'Is the love requited or unrequited?'

'Definitely requited. Oh yes, very requited . . . There will be lots of sex, but very distinguished. We will do the sex beautifully. Isn't it?'

So that is what they did. In fact, over the course of the next few years Erdal wrote two novels under Tiger's name, somehow managing to translate his sexual fantasies and ludicrous plot ideas into something that would satisfy his literary ambitions. And she did manage to do the sex beautifully. It was never extravagant enough for Tiger – though perhaps I should say here that some sensitive readers may find the extracts she quotes, though essential to the progress of the story as she chronicles her hilarious word-by-word negotiations with him, rather too explicit for comfort.

But both novels were respectfully reviewed. By now Tiger had a reputation as a sophisticated Levantine with an almost mystical understanding of women. 'Themes of love, death, sex and time are dealt with here in a fashion that is essentially the product of a Mediterranean Catholic mind, the same climate that shaped the stance of Lorca and Pasolini,' declared the *Oldie* reviewer – though it's true that another review was simply headlined '*Less Sex Please*'. Altogether it was an astonishing achievement, and nobody knew whose achievement it really was – although suspicions were aired more than once in the columns of *Private Eye*.

By this time Erdal herself had married again and it was becoming increasingly difficult to fit her two – or should I say three – lives together. Tiger now had a weekly column in a tabloid newspaper – high-profile women again! – and had installed a dedicated phone line on which he could contact her day or night. Though she was reliant on the work financially, the honesty of her new relationship forced her to take a hard look at what she was doing and what it was doing to her: 'Something I learned as a ghost was that there is an interesting connection between deception and self-deception,' she writes. 'Lying to others plays a vital role in lying to yourself.'

Tiger was in trouble too. It had never been clear where all the money came from and suddenly it seemed it had run out. Backers were sought, and Tiger's extravagant lifestyle was dramatically reduced. There was one grim final journey to the Frankfurt Book Fair and it was there in the hotel, before they parted, that Erdal had an unexpected, poignant glimpse of another Tiger, the one behind the elaborate mask that he habitually wore.

Ghosting is a very funny book. It is also subtle and many-layered, not just the story of the years Erdal spent in a form of slavery to the outrageous, impossible, yet in many ways admirable Tiger, but an account too of a chilly childhood in which she was taught to suppress her own natural voice. It speaks of memory and loss and the masks that most of us wear, and it tells you a lot about the process of writing. The threads are lightly and skilfully drawn together, and it's easy to see why Tiger's literary career was such a success.

Why did she write it? Other ghosts have written books, but by convention it is generally a secret occupation. And what about Tiger? Though Erdal's portrayal of him is unsparing, it's not without affection. In the end the temptation to speak in her own voice and give her own account of events must have been overwhelming. By the time she decided to break with Tiger, Erdal says, 'I was building up a quiet fury at every new demand . . . Psychologists call this emotional dissonance, pretending to feel one thing when you experience another – and it is bad for you, so they say.' Perhaps it is this that gives the book its tremendous force, but whatever the reasons, *Ghosting* is an extraordinary story brilliantly told and one you're not likely to forget.

Before she became co-editor of *Slightly Foxed* HAZEL WOOD ghosted several books, but she never met a Tiger.

Jennie Erdal's *Ghosting* (304pp) is now available in a limited, numbered cloth-bound edition of 2,000 copies (subscriber price: UK & Eire £17, Overseas £19; non subscriber price: UK & Eire £18.50, Overseas £20.50). All prices include post and packing. Copies may be ordered by post (53 Hoxton Square, London N1 6PB), by phone (020 7033 0258) or via our website www.foxedquarterly.com.

A Peak Experience

RICHARD CROCKATT

If literary critics are to be believed, understanding literature requires an analytical approach. We all know, however, that our experience of a particular book or author is often bound up with where we happen to be in life. In that sense, reading is as much about self-discovery as discovery of what the author meant. Perhaps the great books are those which can accommodate the widest possible range of reader experiences of whatever time and place. Certainly the circumstances in which I read Thomas Mann's *The Magic Mountain* (1924) bore little relation to those of its first German readers in the era of the Weimar Republic. Yet connections emerged in the most surprising ways.

In late August 1969 I arrived in St Louis, Missouri, from the UK to embark upon a postgraduate degree in literature. Washington University had a fine pedigree – its founder was T. S. Eliot's grand-father – and a reputation as the 'Harvard of the Midwest'. Among recent appointments to the teaching staff was the eminent poet Howard Nemerov. Knowing the name but little else about him, I signed up for a course of 'independent study' which meant meeting him once a week to discuss a mutually agreed selection of books. Since my chief interest was American poetry, and Nemerov was among the leading living poets, our syllabus chose itself: we would start with the early twentieth-century greats – Ezra Pound, T. S. Eliot, Wallace Stevens, William Carlos Williams – and work down to the present.

Thomas Mann, *The Magic Mountain* (1924) · Trans. H. T. Lowe-Porter
Vintage · Pb · 752pp · £10.99 · ISBN 9780749386429

After a few weeks it became apparent that Nemerov was bored with these poets, and perhaps with me too. I confronted him: 'You don't seem very interested in these people. Perhaps we should read something else.' 'What do you suggest?' he asked. I proposed Thomas Mann. I had read some of the shorter works such as *Tonio Kröger* and *Death in Venice* and also his late masterpiece *Dr Faustus*, a work probably better left till later in life but which, despite my dim understanding, had given me an appetite for Mann's preoccupation with big ideas and in particular the demonic in human experience. 'How about *The Magic Mountain?*' I said. Nemerov's face lit up in a way it had never done with the poets. Only later did I find out why.

Over the next four or five days I read H. T. Lowe-Porter's translation in what I can only describe as a trance. It remains the most intense and absorbing reading experience I have ever had. I lived inside this book and came out the other side feeling a vivid identification with the world it portrayed. It was a milestone in my experience of life no less than of literature, a kind of coming of age, and indeed *The Magic Mountain* is in the great German tradition of the *Bildungsroman*.

Precisely how the discussions with Professor Nemerov went I hardly remember, but I must surely have calmed down and done what students of literature are supposed to do, which is to analyse 'the text' with some detachment, presumably more or less as follows.

The story is simple in outline. A young, recently qualified engineer called Hans Castorp travels from his home in Hamburg to a sanatorium in the Swiss Alps to visit his cousin Joachim who has been a patient there for six months. Castorp had planned a three-week visit but stays for seven years as a resident-cum-patient. He surrenders more or less gracefully to his new reality, becoming a citizen of an alternative world, far removed from 'the flatlands down below' whence he had come.

His native curiosity renders him alert to certain unexpected attractions of the place. The sanatorium houses a collection of remarkable characters whose combined effect is to provide Castorp with an

education, not least the quintessential Enlightenment humanist Herr Settembrini, and the dark Jesuitical apostle of irrationality Herr Naphtha. In his discussions with these imposing individuals Castorp is pulled one way and another by arguments over the deepest moral and intellectual questions in Western civilization.

And of course Castorp falls in love, though it brings as much frustration as anything else. Along the way, he encounters two peak experiences, first of the *Walpurgisnacht* (or Night of the Witches), which is in effect a celebration of the death force, and second, an intense, dream-like vision which comes to him as he is lost in a snow-storm. Here the lesson is a positive one of seizing hold of life. In the light of these experiences the 'lessons' of Settembrini and Naphtha look inadequate and abstract. Indeed the whole sanatorium experience comes to seem lacking in life, and it is life, in the form of news of impending war down in the 'flatlands', which finally prompts Castorp's decision to leave the sanatorium and rejoin the human stream. He joins it just as the First World War is beginning and we are left at the end with a glimpse of him in the thick of battle surrounded by other young men going, presumably, to their deaths.

There are so many layers to this novel that even several readings fail to exhaust them. Yet the spark which lit the whole book for me on first reading was the figure of Hans Castorp, the seeker after light in a world of darkness. This is where we move from the realm of literary criticism to that of self-discovery. Is it so surprising that a somewhat impressionable 21-year-old, seeking answers to the big questions, and suddenly plunged into a different world, should experience an affinity with Hans Castorp? My world bore little relation to the Swiss sanatorium in which Hans Castorp found himself; nor did I linger seven years in the university. Yet I too was engaged in a struggle to come to terms with life. In my case, besides the usual confusions of early adulthood, it took the form of deep dissatisfaction with the studies to which I had apparently committed myself and a related sense that they bore little connection to the 'real world'. That world was in turmoil over the Vietnam War and the society which had produced it. The classroom where I read the great authors was my sanatorium; of the world outside I knew very little. The gap was unbearable, the solution obvious – I had to leave my ivory tower, get out there and try to understand what was happening. After one semester at Washington University I dropped out. I had to participate.

Of course, I cannot say *The Magic Mountain* led me to abandon academe. Nothing is ever that simple. What it did, I think, was to nudge me in a direction I was going already, but in a way that provided me with an intellectual justification for my decision. Leaving the comfortable walls of the university was a positive way forward, not an abandonment. I didn't go to war like Hans Castorp but I did engage with a more or less chaotic world in which my future was uncertain. In short, what stuck with me from the novel was Hans Castorp's decision to take action, which had the liberating effect of breaking the spell that bound him to the lifeless life of the sanatorium.

And then, sometime after I had finished studying with Nemerov, I stumbled on an essay by Thomas Mann on the making of *The Magic Mountain*, published in America in the 1950s and reprinted as an afterword to my edition of the novel. In it Mann refers to a young scholar, Howard Nemerov, who had written a prize-winning undergraduate essay on the theme of 'The Quester Hero in the Works of Thomas Mann'. 'Young Nemerov's is a most able and charming commentary,' Mann wrote, 'and it considerably refreshed my memory and my consciousness of myself.' Nemerov was just 20 when his essay won the prestigious 1940 Bowdoin Prize at Harvard University. Within the year, well before the United States entered the Second World War, Nemerov had joined the Canadian airforce to fight Hitler and then, when America entered the war in December 1941, transferred to the US airforce as a fighter pilot.

Nemerov did not, like Castorp, disappear into the mists of battle. Nor do I have any way of knowing whether he shared my sense of the significance of Hans Castorp's decision to act. What is clear is that Nemerov identified strongly with the quest at the heart of *The Magic Mountain* and also that he went to war, not as a conscript but as a volunteer. The Nemerov I met was approaching 50 but in thinking about his essay written thirty years before, I was suddenly and sharply aware of fellowship with the younger Nemerov as well as with Hans Castorp – youthful seekers all after the grail of truth and understanding. I also now knew why Professor Nemerov's face had lit up at my suggestion that we should read *The Magic Mountain*.

This article was the joint winner of the 2018 *Slightly Foxed* writers' competition. After the experiences described above RICHARD CROCKATT spent several years working in bookshops and as an English teacher but eventually returned to academic life, retiring in 2011 as Professor of American History at the University of East Anglia.

Growing up Edwardian

ANTHONY GARDNER

I wonder if I have ever stayed in an English house that didn't contain a creased and dog-eared book by Osbert Lancaster. In my childhood his collections of pocket cartoons were always a disappointment: the comic sketches on their covers promised hilarity, but the jokes inside – no doubt wonderfully topical in their day – meant little to me. His architectural books, which I noticed as I grew older, seemed forbiddingly esoteric. Not until I acquired parents-in-law who owned almost his entire oeuvre did I discover the memoirs that convinced me of his brilliance: *All Done from Memory* (1953) and *With an Eye to the Future* (1967) are remarkable not just for their wit and powers of observation, but for their highly individual take on Britain's path to two world wars.

It is during the night-time air raids of the summer of 1944 that *All Done from Memory* begins. Rather than await his fate indoors, Lancaster wanders the empty streets of west London, revisiting the scenes of his Edwardian childhood. Notting Hill, where his family once lived, has long been abandoned by the wealthier classes and become a land of seedy flats and bedsits; his book, he tells us, should be seen not primarily as autobiography but as 'a memorial plaque to a vanished world'. The fact that in our own time Notting Hill has been reclaimed by the rich (though not always with respect for its original architecture) adds a dash of irony to his endeavour.

At the heart of the book is a series of portraits of characters from

---

Osbert Lancaster, *All Done from Memory* (1953) and *With an Eye to the Future* (1967), are out of print but we can obtain second-hand copies.

his childhood, each brimming with eccentricity and occasionally certifiable madness (as in the case of the clergyman who tells his largely female congregation that heaven has no place for women). There is Cousin Jenny, who lives in a Victorian time-warp, obsessed with European royalty; Mrs Ullathorne, once a beauty at the court of Napoleon III, her hands 'criss-crossed with the purple hawsers of her veins'; and, most disturbingly, Colonel Hook, whose study – stuffed with mementos of colonial campaigns – betrays a top brass quite unprepared for the mechanized horrors of the imminent Great War.

Lancaster has an almost Trollopian sense of social gradations, and deftly analyses the decline of the urban upper-middle class to which his family belonged. (The invention of the motor car, he explains, tempted people away to the country at weekends, so destroying a pattern of city life which was focused on the local church.) But while he claims that all children are snobs, it is working people who most cheer the young Osbert's world – 'A mother's love is all very well,' he declares, 'but it is a poor substitute for good relations with the cook.' Among the supporting characters are an Italian organ-grinder with his monkey, Kate the housemaid with her fund of political slogans, and 'the old gentleman who came out on winter evenings to play the harp by the foggy radiance of the street lamp'. It's significant that each chapter takes its title from a popular song, for the one thing that people from all walks of life share is a passion for the music-hall.

The onset of war in 1914 is given a rare nuance by his family's love of all things German. His mother's ancestors were immigrants from Hesse, while the Lancasters prided themselves on speaking the language fluently and found in Germans 'all those virtues that they most admired – discipline, industry, physical courage and simple, unaffected Evangelical piety'. When hostilities begin, on Osbert's sixth birthday, he and his parents are at the seaside, and the first thing he notices is the mysterious absence from the beach of four plump bandsmen in Prussian uniforms who would normally be playing extracts from *Tannhäuser*.

His memories of the war itself are few, but the opening chapter of *With an Eye to the Future* evokes a London overwhelmed by gloom, made still deeper by his father's death in action. Even when writing of his darkest moments, however, his humour is never dampened for long: sent to a Swiss TB clinic with strict rules on alcohol, he notes in the dimples of melting snow 'the tell-tale necks of the bottles lightly cast from upper windows during the winter storms'.

He is above all a master of the elegant, periphrastic sentence steeped in gentle irony – never more tellingly deployed than in this description of his difficult mother:

> Partly, perhaps, because of a lonely childhood passed mainly in the company of her elders, and partly thanks to a lifelong inability to suffer fools gladly, and admittedly in some measure due to the unshakeable conviction that she knew far better than those concerned what made for true happiness, my mother's circle was always small and steadily contracted as the years went by and her attitude to life became more managerial.

But he is also adept at the swift, acerbic aside: Sybil Thorndike plays Joan of Arc as 'a particularly maddening Girl Guide at a rather difficult stage of her development', while on the Riviera the gossip columnist Elsa Maxwell lurks 'like Grendel's mother in her mere, ready to pounce on the first worthwhile celebrity to swim past'.

His powers of description are equally impressive. As an artist as well as a writer, he has an extraordinary eye for detail and awareness of different perspectives. He notes, for example, that the mouth is far more revealing than the eyes, and that the surest hallmarks of an era are not its fashions or buzzwords but its gestures – 'a particular fluttering of the hand or trick of standing'. A crowd of churchgoers are defined by their hats ('a mass of elaborate, pale-shaded millinery'); an Oxford don is characterized by his furniture ('suits of Japanese armour in which whole families of mice had made their homes'); and a well-travelled relative by his esoteric collection of ornaments ('masterpieces of tortured ingenuity'). Lancaster is especially fascinated by uniforms, with their many varieties of epaulette and aiguillette – though this does not blind him to the preening vanity of their occupants.

With an Eye to the Future follows a stricter chronology than *All Done from Memory*, taking us from the end of the First World War to the beginning of the Second, with Lancaster progressing from prep school to Charterhouse, then Oxford and the Slade, before embarking on his career as an illustrator. But, as in the earlier book, he has little interest in analysing his own development, preferring to chronicle the *Zeitgeist*; when he does write about himself, it is with the same amused irony he applies to others.

He has particular fun with the craze for the occult which characterized the beginning of the century. His mother was among the many seekers of 'Hidden Wisdom', and an enthusiastic reader of magazines which peddled it. *The National Messenger and Banner* was a favourite, counting an implausible number of naval officers among its contributors and rich with 'that certain knowledge which a close study of the Great Pyramid alone afforded'.

He is more indulgent towards the 1920s – a decade whose frivolity, he argues, was outweighed by its creative vitality, with Diaghilev's Ballets Russes to the fore. As a chronicler of taste he has few rivals, and although Evelyn Waugh had left Oxford by the time Lancaster arrived, the 'Varsity Drag' chapter of *With an Eye to the Future* can almost be read as a glossary to *Brideshead Revisited*, explaining the students' shifting enthusiasms. It has its own cast of memorable characters, including the racing man who summons an invigilator during Finals to place his bets on the 2.30 at Newbury, and a clutch of poets: Louis MacNeice with his 'air of bored and slightly arrogant detachment'; Stephen Spender, 'type-cast for the young Apollo golden-haired, a role to which he brought all the touching grace of a dancing bear'; and John Betjeman, resembling 'a rather down-at-heel Tractarian hymn-writer recently unfrocked'.

If the book has a hero, it is one whose reputation epitomizes the vagaries of history: Lancaster's schoolfriend Ronnie Cartland, long since eclipsed by his eccentric sister Barbara (who appears here as a seductive flapper) and her sentimental novels. Irresistibly charming, deeply sophisticated and prodigiously energetic, Ronnie seemed the personification of a Bright Young Thing; but he also possessed a deeply serious side, 'distinguishing him in the final analysis from the typical Saki hero on whom he might have been thought to have modelled himself'. Elected as a Tory MP at just 28, he was to make his name in the Munich Crisis as a courageous enemy of appeasement, only to be killed in action two years later.

Lancaster himself professes little interest in politics, which makes his observations on the darkening mood of the 1930s all the more intriguing: while the First World War caught most people by surprise, the auguries that preceded the Second were hard to miss. His social engagements include a dance given by Diana Mosely for her sister Unity Mitford in 1932, the atmosphere of which brings 'a presentiment of coming, and probably unwelcome, change' – confirmed by the sight of a comatose Augustus John being carried out by two footmen. The age of aesthetes has given way to that of politicians.

Extraordinarily, though, passion for German culture runs high among Lancaster's friends until well into the decade, fostered in part by guilt over the punitive terms of the Treaty of Versailles. Moreover,

he explains, 'such radical movements as those represented by Kurt Weill and George Grosz . . . encouraged the belief that there was a reliable, built-in opposition to the nightmare ascendancy of lower middle-class nationalism'. The delight with which sophisticated Germans greet Hitler's accession comes as a profound shock, as does the appetite for appeasement among British grandees. The book ends, artfully, back where Lancaster's story began in the streets of west London, as the news comes through that Poland has been invaded.

The writing is only part of the memoirs' allure, for both volumes are of course peppered with Lancaster's enchanting illustrations. One of my favourites shows a dozen tiny schoolboys being led along the seafront at Littlehampton: none is given facial features, yet each miraculously has his own personality. Elsewhere we see the infant Osbert being doted on by women in enormous hats; a gallery of dim-witted monarchs encrusted with orders of chivalry; tweedy dons and menacing lap-dogs. All are, as illustrations should be, a distillation of the books' beguiling prose – reminding us that, in a dangerous world, an eye for mankind's absurdity is an invaluable aid to survival.

ANTHONY GARDNER is the author of two novels, *Fox* and *The Rivers of Heaven*, and a collection of poetry, *The Pool and Other Poems*. The architecture of his youth ranged from Pont Street Dutch to Irish Georgian; he now divides his time between Twentieth-Century Functional and Edwardian Redbrick.

Forest School

HELENA DRYSDALE

In most childhood games, the first thing you need to do is eliminate the parents. You can't be an outlaw or have adventures if you have parents to spoil the excitement. My sisters and I were often on the run or in hiding, and for that we had to be orphans. Our best hideaway was a ratty loft floored with bantam droppings, where we constructed a den out of old packing cases and smoked pipes stuffed with the white pith from inside reed stalks. We would pull up the ladder, and our parents never came near us.

All the best children's writers understand this and get rid of the parents as soon as possible. J. K. Rowling makes Harry Potter an orphan, housed in a cupboard under the stairs by the awful Dursleys. C. S. Lewis evacuates the Pevensey children from London during the Second World War to stay with an old Professor, whose spare-room wardrobe is the portal to Narnia; their parents never feature. The British Empire provided ample opportunities for such scenarios. Aged 6, Kipling was packed off from India to Southsea to board with a brutal foster family, as immortalized in his tragic story 'Baa Baa, Black Sheep' (1888). In Frances Hodgson Burnett's *A Little Princess* (1905) and *The Secret Garden* (1911), the young heroines Sara Crew and Mary Lomax – both spoilt, and sickly from the climate – return from India to make their way in England, parentless and alone.

Another powerful motivation in my childhood was to get out of school. Anything to avoid watery fish on Fridays or being smacked over the head for making a mistake in maths. Later, as a boarding-school teenager regularly punished for 'dumb insolence', my aim was to get out of church, to which we went in crocodile, wearing green pill-box hats. One Sunday some friends and I answered the register, then sidled behind a curtain; while the rest of the school trudged off down the main road we spent a blissful hour or two roaming the woods.

The magic of such adventures is captured in one of the great children's books, BB's *Brendon Chase*, first published in 1944 but set thirty or so years earlier. It's the end of the Easter holidays, and Robin, John and Harold Hensman can't face returning to their boarding-school. Their 'people' are in India, and for years they've been entrusted to the care of their fussy maiden aunt, assisted by the vicar. Banchester isn't bad as English public schools go, but they are country boys who dread being trapped in a classroom when summer approaches and the great outdoors calls. They hatch a plan. They will escape and hide out like Robin Hood and his merry men in the eleven-thousand-acre forest of Brendon Chase.

This they do for all of one summer, autumn and winter, living feral in a hollow oak, defying not only parents and school, but society generally – the national press, the police, the church, outraged locals, conformity, class and, above all, the superficial niceties of urban civilization. Like Henry Thoreau's *Walden, or Life in the Woods*, theirs is a declaration of independence, a voyage of self-discovery, a satire and a sort of manual of self-sufficiency and bushcraft, as well as a rip-roaring tale of hide-and-seek. Above all it is a poetic evocation of the natural world, shot through with nostalgia for the freedom and simplicity of childhood, and for unwrecked pre-First World War rural England.

BB is famous for his tales of the last gnomes of England, particularly the Carnegie Medal-winning *The Little Grey Men* (see *SF* no. 55). In that book and its sequel, *Down the Bright Stream*, three brothers leave home and survive in the wild on luck, their wits and their hunting skills. While the mouse-size gnomes are immersed in nature, personally confronting its hazards, to me the reality of the Hensman brothers made *Brendon Chase* equally – if not more – compelling. I was too big and clumping to travel as the gnomes did up the Folly Brook by coracle, but I could imagine living like the brothers in a hollow oak, trapping rabbits and swimming in the Blind Pool.

My mother gave me *Brendon Chase* for my eighth birthday, and I reread it so often that the cover shredded. Even in 1968 its world seemed dated – the boys say 'Rot!' and 'By Jove!', and happily rob the nest of a rare honey buzzard. Their attitude towards 'the fair sex' is equally questionable: Aunt Ellen – who employs a cook, a governess, a gardener, a morning maid and a 'tweeny' – provides insufferable 'petticoat' government. But I accepted that the book was of its time, and its descriptions of the countryside are as vivid today as they ever were – more so, given how much of it is now buried under tarmac.

Brendon Chase is also full of memorable characters. 'The Whiting' is an absent-minded vicar so passionate about entomology that he forgets everything in pursuit of an elusive Wood White or a Purple Emperor. Then there's old Smokoe Joe, a gruff charcoal-burner with a gargantuan nose who lives in the Chase; and the boys' nemesis, the ponderous local bobby, Sergeant Bunting. In a wonderful scene Bunting, humiliated by his failure to catch the boys, cycles on a sweltering summer's day into the Chase – convinced they are hiding there *somewhere* – and decides to cool off in the Blind Pool. He removes his helmet and frees his feet from their sweaty prisons, poses on the end of a log, naked, white and pot-bellied, and plunges in. He turns on his back and floats, staring into the summer blue. It's heaven. He emerges to find . . . well, I won't spoil it. But imagine a policeman cycling ten miles home in nothing but helmet, boots and white gloves.

Of course, the book's main focus is on the fugitives themselves, their relationships with each other, and how they grow and change during their adventures. They overcome their own fears and discover things about themselves. They squabble and occasionally fight, but they share solid British values of fair play, honour and pluck. We follow them as they learn how to shoot and become skilled at fishing, tracking, snaring and skinning. They grow alert, sharp-eyed, almost subsumed in nature. But this is not over-idealized: times are hard when winter arrives, and they often miss the domestic world.

On a midnight foray back to the Dower House for supplies, Robin grabs Thoreau's *Walden*, and Richard Jefferies' *The Amateur Poacher* and *Bevis: The Story of a Boy*. Big John takes *Huckleberry Finn*, and Little John, aka Harold, the youngest at 12, *Tom Sawyer*. All these were BB's favourites. In some ways *Brendon Chase* is a portrait of his own childhood, as described in his autobiography *A Child Alone* (1978). As a boy (born in 1905) he was considered too delicate to be sent away to boarding-school, so he grew up roaming around the Northamptonshire countryside alone with his BB wildfowling gun (hence his pseudonym), nesting, fishing and poaching. Robin, the eldest at 15, is most like him, a thoughtful, solitary boy who likes nothing more than to wander alone, lost in a kind of ecstatic stupor.

Like Thoreau and Jefferies, BB writes precisely and beautifully about nature, and nature lies at the core of the book. When the Reverend Whiting goes butterfly hunting in Brendon Chase, we share his excitement.

> The meadow browns were hatching, they were bob, bobbing everywhere, nothing but meadow browns, drab meadow browns. They sat on the warm grass and seemed to look at him out of their cheeky painted eyes at the tips of their wings . . . And then . . . he saw it, quite suddenly he saw it, the glorious regal insect of his dreams!

The Purple Emperor is flying down a ride, then soaring heaven-wards to the top of an oak. 'There he watched it, flitting round one of the topmost sprays far out of reach, mocking him, the Unattainable, the Jewel, the King of butterflies!' BB went on to be pivotal in the conservation of the Purple Emperor. Unlike the vegetarian Thoreau, he described himself as a 'countryman', by which he meant not just observing and exploring, but being active in country pursuits. He saw no contradiction between loving nature, conserving it and killing it, because the killing involved becoming like the creature he stalked, behaving like it, and steeping himself in its ways. He was a hunter-gatherer, killing only for the pot.

In *Brendon Chase* he unflinchingly portrays the gutting or 'drawing' of birds and rabbits, and when the boys kill and butcher a pig there is no horror or squeamishness. This is about survival, and expertise. You singe the pig's hairs, grind down a salt lick you steal from a field, dig out a hollow trunk, fill it with water, dissolve the salt lick in it, and steep the pig for seven days. Then you dangle the hams over a fire and smoke them, taking care to do this at night so as not to reveal your location. The result is bacon more delicious than you have ever tasted. BB's knowledge of flora and fauna is equally mani-

fest. He never talks down to his readers, describing and naming each plant and animal in detail. Although as a child I didn't understand it all, I was bewitched by the smells and sounds, the intricate details and the sense of being steeped in a place, watchful and alive, full of wonder.

One of the book's highlights are its illustrations. So few book illustrations capture what the reader imagines, but in this case we trust them because they are by Denys Watkins-Pitchford, who was of course BB himself. After training at Northampton School of Art and the Royal Academy, and briefly in Paris, he was for seventeen years the assistant art master at Rugby, until he took up writing and illustrating full-time. For *Brendon Chase* he used black-and-white scraperboard, a delicate form in which to convey the dappled light and shade of the forest. We see the sun shafting across the trunk of the hollow oak and glancing off the Blind Pool with a tree reflected in its depths. A few deft scratches outline the hirsute pig and John standing over it with his gun, looking both triumphant and sorry. The most dramatic illustration is of Robin climbing a Scots pine in search of the honey buzzard's egg. We look skywards to glimpse him as a tiny figure high in the branches, the nest a bundle of sticks overhead, and we can imagine his vertiginous horror as he surveys the world below him.

The scraperboard is also a perfect medium for the monochrome worlds of night and snow, creating a mysterious, even mystical quality. In fact BB's images are as lively as his text: each feeds the other, and both express his exceptional powers of observation and his bond with the natural world. His father was a vicar, but it was in nature, it seems, that he put his own faith, even when, poignantly, he saw that world diminishing under his gaze.

HELENA DRYSDALE is a writer living in rural Somerset, where she hopes one day to see a Purple Emperor.

BB's *Brendon Chase* (288pp), including its original black-and-white illustrations, is available from Slightly Foxed in a new limited cloth-bound edition of 2,000 copies (subscriber price: UK & Ireland £17; Overseas £18; non-subscriber price: UK & Ireland £19; Overseas £21). All prices include post and packing. Copies may be ordered by post (53 Hoxton Square, London N1 6PB), by phone (020 7033 0258) or via our website www. foxedquarterly.com.

Trollope's Ireland

MARGARET DRABBLE

I have been reading Trollope's fiction over several decades, but it was not until this year that I embarked upon his three principal Irish novels. They have not been his most popular works, and I, like many others, was deterred by the heavy use of dialect which slows the reader down and makes the page look unwelcoming. But when I decided to overcome this prejudice, I was rewarded. It didn't take long to convert me: the first paragraphs of his very first novel, *The Macdermots of Ballycloran* (1847), have a peculiar magic. The narrator Trollope (who is soon subsumed into his tale) tells us, in what was to become his characteristically intimate tone, that he found himself at a loss for after-dinner entertainment when stranded by business (in the author's case this would have been Post Office business) in the 'quiet little village of Drumsna', on a bend in the Shannon, about seventy miles north-west of Dublin. 'Now, in such a situation, to take a walk is all the brightest man can do, and the dullest always does the same. There is a kind of gratification in seeing what one has never seen before, be it ever so little worth seeing; and the gratification is the greater if the chances be that one will never see it again.' This is a wonderfully inviting opening. This is a man for whom life is an adventure, a perpetual exploration.

By chance and through ignorance of the neighbourhood he walks in the wrong direction, away from the pretty picturesque bridge and

---

The Macdermots of Ballycloran (1847), *The Kellys and the O'Kellys* (1848), *Castle Richmond* (1860), *An Eye for an Eye* (1879) and *The Landleaguers* (1883) are available in print-on-demand editions but we can obtain good second-hand copies.

Julia Margaret Cameron
© National Portrait Gallery

woods and along 'as dusty, ugly and disagreeable a road as is to be found in any county in Ireland', but this unpromising beginning brings him to the subject that inspired him: the immensely decayed but once grand house of a Connaught gentleman. The building, into which he makes his way, is open to the elements, and the effects of Time and Ruin are described with a poetic intensity – the roof was off, the windows and window frames and 'everything that wanted keeping had gone': the joists and beams were 'ready to fall, like the skeleton of a felon left to rot on an open gibbet', and the gardens were half covered with potato heaps.

The story of the tragic fall of the house of Ballycloran is told to the narrator by the guard of the coach that drives him away from Drumsna to Boyle. It is a tale of a family descending inevitably towards disaster, set in the 1830s against a background of political agitation, religious strife, heavy drinking and poverty. This was the time of Ribbonism, when Catholic working men formed illegal secret societies to bind themselves by oath to resist their landlords and to protest against ejection for non-payment of rent, and ribbon men feature in the plot. The principal characters are Thaddeus (Thady) Macdermot and his sister Euphemia, known as Feemy. They are the children of ageing and impotent Larry Macdermot, who is unable to manage his dwindling estate and finds himself at the mercy of unscrupulous lawyers and agents.

Feemy, a romantic girl of 20, is in love with the enemy, in the person of the dashing but untrustworthy revenue officer, the Protestant Captain Ussher, who courts her and takes liberties with her but has no fixed intention of marrying her. Despite her slatternly dress, her hair 'fastened up with a bit of old black ribbon and a comb boasting only two teeth', her idleness, her thumb-worn novels and her down-at-heel shoes and her habit of sitting all morning with her feet on the fender, she is a sympathetic as well as a vulnerable figure.

Her brother, the well-meaning but not very resourceful Thady, is also drawn with compassion, and the reader follows him with mounting anxiety as he becomes compromised by his association with a group of local rebels, conspiring to overthrow the hated Ussher. Trollope's depiction of the wedding scene at which the drunken Thady makes a fatal error is masterly; all the Irish ingredients are there – the boiling cabbages and smoking potatoes, the 'huge lumps of blood-red mutton', the sweating bride-cum-cook, the wise and kindly priest, the bashful village lads, the piper playing Irish tunes. There is an authenticity and vigour here that surpass many of Trollope's later English comic low-life passages. Trollope, who spent nearly twenty years there, knew his Ireland.

The denouement is violent and tragic. Feemy dies of a broken heart when Ussher betrays her, and Thady's end is foreshadowed by the image of the gibbet at Ballycloran. I was shocked by the outcome, as I had been expecting some more Trollopian compromise. I admired it, but his early readers did not. Had the book been more successful, might its author have travelled in a different direction? As it was, he apologized for it at the end of *Barchester Towers* (1857), the second novel in his more pleasing clerical saga, telling us that 'A late writer, wishing to sustain his interest to the last page, hung his hero at the end of the third volume. The consequence was that no one would read his novel.'

He had not arrived at this worldly wisdom when he wrote *The Kellys and the O'Kellys* (1848) which, again, is set uncompromisingly in Ireland, at the time of the Repealers and the Dublin trial of John O'Connell in 1843. Again, the political backdrop is vividly realized, but in the foreground are the fortunes of two starkly contrasted heiresses, the simple-minded and domestically oppressed Anastasia 'Anty' Lynch and the strong-willed upper-class beauty Fanny Wyndham. Their social spheres, although poles apart, intersect, and Trollope skilfully analyses the subtleties of class and conduct on a much broader canvas than he attempted with the Macdermots. He takes us from court rooms to castles, from the racecourse to the hunting field, from Morrison's Hotel in Dublin to Mrs Kelly's humble inn in Dunmore. He makes his first attempt to distinguish between the very bad young man and the bad but redeemable young man, telling us confidently that 'Lord Kilcullen was a heartless roué, whereas Lord Ballindine was only a thoughtless rake . . .'

The hospitable but ugly inn, with its large drinking room and rickety chairs, its earthen floor and its dingy, dark kitchen, plays an important role in the novel. 'An Irish kitchen is devoted to hospitality in every sense of the word. Its doors are open to almost all loungers and idlers, and the chances are that Billy Bawn, the cripple, or Judy Molloy, the deaf old hag, are more likely to find the required utensil than the cook herself . . .' It is here that Anty takes refuge when attacked by her violent and bullying brother, who is trying to cheat her out of her modest inheritance. And although Trollope is already showing himself at home with the landed gentry, with titled absentee landlords and rakes and roués, it is Anty's fate that we follow with the greatest interest: will she get to marry the handsome Frank Kelly, younger than she is, eager for her money, but kind at heart, or will she too, like the helpless Feemy, meet a tragic end?

It takes great skill to make so unpromising a heroine as Anty hold our attention, and Trollope keeps us guessing to the end. The plot of his third Irish novel, *Castle Richmond* (1860), is more melodramatic and predictable, again turning on inheritance and disinheritance, and its most powerful scenes are evocations of the Irish famine, which Trollope and his wife witnessed at first hand. He opens his narrative by telling the reader that he knows that Irish novels have gone out of fashion, but he does not make clear why he has returned to this theme: perhaps it was agitated memories of the famine that drew him back. His views on what caused the famine, and why God permitted it, are at best confused, but nonetheless compelling. He is at times satirical about the Irish character and Irish traits, but he is not frivolous or flippant. Had he stayed there, he might have continued to work out this tragic theme. But he came to England, and to worldly success, as did the later hero of his Palliser novels, Phineas Finn.

Trollope was to admit that he had been wrong to make the aspiring politician Phineas an Irish Catholic, and that he had thus voluntarily presented himself with a host of problems, not all of which could be resolved as easily as the question of Phineas's marriage to his first sweetheart, the very Irish Mary Flood Jones. Phineas is true to Mary, despite the odds, but she shortly dies, most conveniently, in childbirth. She is reborn, more tragically, in the protagonist of *An Eye for an Eye* (1879), Kate O'Hara, whose fate echoes that of poor Feemy. Much of this novel is set in Dorset, but the scenes set on the Irish coast where Kate is wooed and won by the handsome English officer Fred Neville have a dramatic intensity. The impossibility of marriage between the daughter of a Catholic widow and the heir to an English earldom becomes increasingly and remorselessly apparent, despite the interventions of the attractively drawn 'wise priest' Father Marty, and all ends badly for everybody.

Those were not Trollope's final thoughts on the country he knew so well. His last novel, like his first, was set in Ireland. *The Landleaguers* was written during his last illness and published posthumously in 1883. He had come full circle. Those years as an English civil servant in a not-quite-foreign land had left an indelible mark. And one cannot help but wonder whether the tenor of his entire output might have been slightly different had *The Macdermots* sold all of the 400 copies that were printed, and been more respectfully received. It is, as he always maintained, a very good book.

After a brief and inglorious career as an actress with the Royal Shakespeare Company MARGARET DRABBLE DBE became a full-time writer, and has written nineteen novels, most recently *The Dark Flood Rises* (2016). She has also written biographies of Arnold Bennett and Angus Wilson, and edited the fifth and sixth editions of the *Oxford Companion to English Literature*.

Mr Polly Walks to Freedom

KEN HAIGH

'I think I'm having a mid-life crisis,' I told my wife the other night at dinner.

Instead of sympathizing, she started laughing, and then immediately apologized. 'I'm sorry, dear. You know I love you, but you're always having a mid-life crisis. You've been having a mid-life crisis since the moment I met you, twenty-seven years ago.'

Now this is more or less true, but I prefer not to hear it. And I think 'always' is a bit of an exaggeration. The fact that my friends call me 'Eeyore' is neither here nor there. But I suppose that's why I've always loved H. G. Wells's novel *The History of Mr Polly*. Polly and I have so much in common.

When we first meet Alfred Polly, he is sitting on a stile between 'two threadbare-looking fields' contemplating suicide:

> Mr Polly sat on the stile and hated the whole scheme of life –
> which was at once excessive and inadequate of him. He hated
> Fishbourne, he hated Fishbourne High Street, he hated his
> shop and his wife and his neighbours – every blessed neighbour
> – and with indescribable bitterness he hated himself.

Seeing no way out, he resolves to kill himself.

This seems a rather unpromising start to a comic novel, but that's exactly what *The History of Mr Polly* is: a comic masterpiece – the sunniest, warmest novel H. G. Wells ever wrote. Certainly, it was his

H. G. Wells, *The History of Mr Polly* (1910)
Penguin · Pb · 272pp · £8.99 · ISBN 9780141441078

least polemical. Later in life, Wells would admit that, if he didn't rank *Polly* as his best book, it was certainly his happiest and the one he cared for most.

Part of the attraction lies in its hero, Alfred Polly. He is a small, inconsequential man, the sort who drifts through life as if in a dream. 'I've never really planned my life, or set out to live,' Polly admits. 'I happened; things happened to me. It's so with everyone.' But Polly is graced with a warm heart and a real need for affection. He has a romantic streak fuelled by a voracious and indiscriminate love of reading. He also has a knack for comic neologism that makes up for his lack of formal education. Pushy youngsters are referred to as a 'Shoveacious Cult', full of 'Smart Juniosity'. A man with a prominent Adam's apple is the 'Soulful Owner' of an 'Exorbiant Largenial Development'. Wells's handling of dialogue and dialect is deft and frequently hilarious. The funerary dinner for Mr Polly's father reads like a Robert Altman script channelled through the muse of Charles Dickens.

Polly is also Wells at his most autobiographical. Like his hero, Wells started life in trade as a draper's apprentice and plunged into an unhappy marriage with a cousin. Like Polly, he had little formal education but loved to read. (Wells would eventually win a government scholarship to a teacher-training college where Darwin's friend T. H. Huxley was one of his instructors.) But here the parallel breaks down. Wells would escape his former life through literary success. Polly, it would seem, must follow a darker path.

But nothing turns out as Polly anticipates. This is a comedy after all. One night when his wife is at church, Polly resolves to cut his throat. He will disguise his suicide by first setting fire to his shop, so that his wife can claim the insurance. But the fire spreads so quickly Polly must delay his own death to rescue a neighbour, a deaf elderly woman, whom he leads across the burning rooftops to safety. His neighbours, fellow shopkeepers with whom he had been carrying on a running feud for years, congratulate him and call him a hero, each dreaming of

the new start that the insurance money will allow. Polly's wife arrives home to find their shop gutted and plots to rebuild on a larger scale. But Polly has had an epiphany: Fishbourne isn't the world, he realizes, and 'If the world does not please you, *you can change it.*' One day, he quietly slips away with just twenty pounds in his pocket and walks out into the Kent countryside and a new life.

Wells clearly loved the English countryside, for he describes it in glowing terms:

There is no countryside like the English countryside for those who have learned to love it; its firm yet gentle lines of hill and dale, its ordered confusion of features, its deer parks and downland, its castles and stately houses, its hamlets and old churches, its farms and ricks and great barns and ancient trees, its pools and ponds and shining threads of rivers, its flower-starred hedgerows, its orchards and woodland patches, its village greens and kindly inns.

He goes on to list the pleasures of other countrysides in other parts of the world and concludes:

But none of these change scene and character in three miles of walking, nor have so mellow a sunlight nor so diversified a cloudland nor confess the perpetual refreshment of the strong soft winds that blow from off the sea, as our mother England does.

No one could write like this if they did not feel it. But for anyone suffering from a continuous mid-life crisis *Mr Polly* is a dangerous book to read, for Polly finds that the vagabond life suits him.

For the first time in many years he had been leading a healthy human life, living constantly in the open air, walking every day for eight or nine hours, eating sparingly, accepting every conversational opportunity, not even disdaining discussion of possible work. And beyond mending a hole in his coat, that he had made while negotiating barbed wire, with a borrowed needle and thread in a lodging house, he had done no real work at all. Neither had he worried about business nor about times and seasons. And for the first time in his life he had seen the Aurora Borealis.

It is not long before Polly has become a larger and better man. After a number of adventures, which include rescuing an old woman and her granddaughter from a dangerous bully, he finds a place as a general handyman in a cosy riverside inn, and he is content.

At the end of the novel, however, Polly's conscience prods him to return home and check on his wife. He discovers, to his surprise, that he is dead. A body has been found in the river, and his wife has claimed it as his, using Polly's life insurance to start a tea shop with her sister. When Polly re-enters her life she is terrified that her fraud will be discovered, but Polly assures her that he is quite happy to remain a corpse, and they part amicably. He returns to the inn, his conscience clear.

Marital strife is rarely concluded with such ease, but then *The History of Mr Polly* is a comedy. Only in fiction do we see such happy endings, and perhaps that is why we read fiction. And which of us has not wished that he could just walk away from his humdrum existence, throw a rucksack over his shoulder and become a vagabond? Richard Jefferies, another writer who celebrated the English countryside, wrote: 'Hardly any of us have but thought, some day I'll go on a voyage; but the years go by, and still we have not sailed.'

Tick, tock.

In his youth, KEN HAIGH wandered the world as an itinerant teacher, working in the Canadian Arctic, China and Bhutan. Today he is a librarian and freelance writer, but he dreams of the day when he can dust off his backpack and resume the vagabond life.

Cogs in a Fighting Machine

HENRY JEFFREYS

While reading Len Deighton's *Bomber* (1970), I was reminded of Solzhenitsyn's line – 'To do evil a human being must first of all believe that what he's doing is good.' *Bomber* is a novel about the area bombing of Germany during the Second World War. Targeting German cities and civilians is a part of Britain's war that is still extremely controversial. It doesn't fit into the heroic narrative of the Battle of Britain, the Blitz or D-Day. Almost alone among British forces, bomber crews were not issued with a campaign medal when the war ended. The debate as to whether the bombing was a necessary evil or simply just evil continues to exercise historians and writers to this day.

Deighton is perhaps uniquely placed to answer the question. By the time he had completed *Bomber*, he probably knew more about the bombing campaign from both the Allied and the Axis perspectives than anybody, for his book was based on years of research. The acknowledgements, with their long list of veterans to whom he spoke, give you some idea of just how much work he put into *Bomber* – he even flew as a passenger in a Heinkel so he could understand what German fighter crews had experienced.

The story takes place over twenty-four hours in June 1943 in three main locations: a British bomber airfield in East Anglia, a German radar station in Holland and a small German town called Altgarten near the Dutch border. The cast is vast but there are a few principal characters around whom the narrative is anchored. On the British

Len Deighton, *Bomber* (1970), is out of print but we can obtain second-hand copies.

side there's Samuel Lambert who pilots a Lancaster bomber known as *The Creaking Door*. Despite captaining the plane, he isn't an officer. In fact he is disliked by some of his seniors because he's not what would now be described as a 'team player' – literally in this case, since he refuses to play for his squadron cricket eleven despite his skill as a bowler. This annoys the Group Captain, a man fond of sporting metaphors who at one point says: 'Cricket's a little like flying in combat . . . long leisurely times in the pavilion followed by a brief moment when a chap faces some fast bowling.' There's something of the Angry Young Man about Lambert in his disdain for this public-school insouciance.

As with other Deighton novels such as *The Ipcress File* (memorably made into a film starring Michael Caine), class permeates the British. The RAF is presented as snobbish and hidebound by rules: 'The English believe that only gentlemen can be leaders,' points out one character. But the class system isn't Lambert's only problem. Early on in the novel, he speaks out against bombing civilian targets and is quickly slapped down. Far more to the taste of the senior officers is Captain Sweet, an unpleasant, scheming figure who lacks Lambert's experience and leadership qualities but who has been regarded as officer material from the day he joined up: 'He had a clear, high voice, energy, enthusiasm and an unquestioning readiness to flatter and defer to the voice of authority.'

The German scenes revolve around August Bach, a widower and commander of the radar station in Holland, whose young family is over the border in Altgarten. He is falling in love with the children's nanny, Anna-Luisa, who is barely out of her teens. Initially she is portrayed as a naïve dreamer but she's not quite all she seems. The other principal Germans include the Mayor of Altgarten, the Burgomaster, who is more preoccupied with organizing his birthday party than with the war, and Löwenherz, an ace fighter pilot whose job it is to intercept RAF bombers. He's from an old military family and is torn between doing his patriotic duty and speaking out against the full horrors of the Nazi regime. Deighton avoids the caricature of heel-clicking Germans. Even those who commit the worst deeds, such as the amoral Viennese doctor Hans Furth, are humanized and even made appealing.

The main plot is simple. A huge force of 400 British aeroplanes flies over to Germany to destroy the industrial city of Krefeld. It is the job of Germans such as Löwenherz and Bach to stop them. However, within that plot lie a swirl of subplots in which characters scheme,

© Imperial War Museum

fall in love and experience personal triumphs and failures; and all the while we are never allowed to forget that every single one of them is a human being. *Bomber's* enormous cast includes airmen, soldiers, firemen, nurses, doctors, wives and civilians of all descriptions. Deighton's skill is in sketching them so deftly that the reader is never confused.

It's not only the characters who have back stories. The sleepy market town of Altgarten is given such a rich history that you will be surprised to learn it is not a real place. Deighton is particularly good at writing about inanimate objects. Each Lancaster bomber, such as the aptly named *Creaking Door*, has its own personality. Julian Symons, a crime writer and contemporary, once remarked that Deighton was the only person he knew who actually liked machines. In *Bomber* the men are merely tiny cogs in a fighting machine. 'It's as though the plane goes to bomb Germany of its own predatory volition, as though it takes us along just for the ride,' explains one character.

Men and machines come together in a cinematic climax. The switches between Germany, Holland and Britain that had taken place over chapters now take place over paragraphs or even lines. Deighton describes aerial combat thus: 'three groups of men using every device that science could invent began to grope around the blackness like gunmen in a sewer'. If intercepting aircraft is a haphazard affair then precision aerial bombing is a chimera. The British plan quickly unravels. A German fighter shoots down a British light aircraft. The crew jettison their marker bombs over Altgarten rather than over the industrial city of Krefeld. The British are convinced they have the right target because on radar Altgarten's greenhouses look like enormous factories.

As the bombs fall and explode among the town's wooden houses, a dry wind whips up a firestorm. Deighton's description of a town being destroyed building by building is a tour de force. Area bombing as practised by the Allies is presented in horrific detail: 'even after the last of the bombers had departed the effectiveness of the fire-fighting and salvage teams would be hampered by the delayed-action bombs. They would continue to explode for two more days.' Those few who survive are terribly damaged: 'it was the beginning of a mental breakdown from which they would never recover'.

Rather as in *Game of Thrones*, characters with whom we have engaged are discarded with shocking suddenness and often appalling violence. Kokke, a German pilot, is killed by a bird through the windscreen: 'it was impossible to distinguish where the bird's remains ended and Kokke's face began'. Another major character survives the raid only to die in a motorcycle accident after he has landed. Deighton follows his characters' thoughts to the bitter end; there is even an epilogue in which the surviving characters' lives are sketched in a way that is both bathetic and peculiarly moving: 'Peterson lives in Montreal and is vice-president of a small company that makes camping equipment.'

Bomber is also at times a very funny novel: 'You don't believe in this war,' says Cohen, one of a Lancaster's crew. 'Believe in it? . . . you make it sound like a rumour,' Lambert replies. The Viennese doctor Hans Furth is described as 'nibbling the German language like sachertorte'; Gerda Pippert, who gatecrashes the Burgomaster's dinner in Altgarten, thinks it 'the most exciting prospect she could remember since her holiday in Heidelberg in 1938'; and Voss, a German tailor, muses: 'Some people said things against them, but the Nazis had done wonders for the uniform business, whatever other faults they might have.'

We are used to the First World War being depicted as bleak but the popular view of the British role in the Second is largely the creation of stirring films such as *The Dam Busters* or sentimental songs. In *Bomber* there are no patriotic clichés and nobody is ennobled by war.

At the end of the novel the surviving British bombers return to East Anglia. The crews congratulate themselves on a job well done but a lowly WAAF corporal looks at the photos taken from the aircraft and realizes they have missed their target. The men are going to have to go back on the next clear night and finish the job. This ending also reminded me of Solzhenitsyn and his *One Day in the Life of Ivan Denisovich* which depicts the struggle to survive just one day in the Gulag. *Bomber* shows only one day in one small theatre of the war. Tomorrow there will be more bombing raids, not just over Germany, but over other parts of occupied Europe and over Japan. The horrors of a botched raid on a town such as Altgarten won't even get a mention in the history books. Deighton leaves the reader to make up his or her own mind about the morality of area bombing. In *Bomber* he is simply saying, this is how it was, and it's impossible to argue with that.

HENRY JEFFREYS' book *Empire of Booze: British History through the Bottom of a Glass* was published in 2016.

Grinning at the Devil

KATE TYTE

In my university English literature seminar group, we used to complain about historical fiction that suffered from 'The Bakelite knob
problem'. It read like an antiques catalogue, full of unintentionally
hilarious descriptions of everyday things. Yet while the Bakelite
knobs and corset fastenings of history can be over-imagined in
historical fiction, psychological difference is often overlooked. There
are endless historical stories with proto-feminist heroines, politically
correct heroes and bigoted, moustache-twiddling villains.

Isak Dinesen's *Seven Gothic Tales*, published in 1934 but set a hundred years earlier, doesn't feature any distracting Bakelite knobs.
Dinesen's past is not full of furniture: it is an operatic stage-set of
budding forests and frozen seas, jagged mountains and dusty roads.
Treading the boards is a cast of characters with a pre-Freudian psychology as remote and alien from us as the mysterious creatures that
scuttle in darkness across the ocean floors. The past is not another
country: it is a different world.

Seven Gothic Tales is an apt title. All tales must have a teller, and
Dinesen's seven separate tales – all long, some long enough to be
novellas – have multiple storytellers. There are tales within tales
within tales, each opening on to the next like a series of Russian dolls.
The themes are Gothic: doomed love affairs; the inevitability of fate;
supernatural forces. There are gloomy monasteries, ghosts, violent
murders and bizarre plot twists including a nun who transforms into

---

Isak Dinesen, *Seven Gothic Tales* (1934), is out of print but we can obtain
second-hand copies.

a monkey. But if you are looking for horror, this is the wrong book for you. There are very few blood-curdling screams here and a complete absence of cellars or instruments of torture: in Dinesen's hands, the Gothic is more an atmosphere.

With its macabre spectacles and heightened emotions Gothic fiction can sometimes be dismissed as unreal and bombastic. Yet behind the grand edifice of the Gothic castle is there not a sort of reality? Don't we all experience thwarted passions, dashed hopes and howling despair? By elevating suffering into something beautiful, the Gothic provides us with a safe space in which to wallow in misery. Fantasy and excess take the edges off life's worst aspects. In 'The Dreamers', a storyteller asks his listeners, 'What is a man, when you come to think upon him, but a minutely set, ingenious machine for turning, with infinite artfulness, the red wine of Shiraz into urine?' This statement is both depressingly true and ridiculous. Here we can safely indulge in a penchant for melodrama, and revel in the glorious absurdity of it.

Isak Dinesen was born Karen Dinesen to a wealthy family, in Denmark, in 1885. Her beloved father committed suicide when she was 10. In her twenties she fell madly in love with one of her cousins. He rejected her so she married his twin brother. Karen's second-best husband made her a baroness, took her to Kenya, where they started a coffee plantation, and infected her with syphilis in the first year of their marriage. The coffee plantation was a long-drawn-out disaster, as related in her well-known memoir *Out of Africa*. By 1931 Baroness Blixen's marriage had failed, the business had failed, and she was suffering excruciating pain from the syphilis and the poisonous mercury used to treat it. And her lover, an upper-class Englishman and big-game hunter, had just been killed in a plane crash.

Karen returned to Denmark and moved back in with her mother. She was disgraced and debilitated, but she did not despair. She wrote. For Karen, a life well lived was a courageous life. And her brand of courage was a magnificent, swaggering bravado in the face of death, like the Charge of the Light Brigade. *Seven Gothic Tales* was soon complete – written in English, on the grounds that there was a bigger market for English-language books than Danish ones. It was rejected by publishers until one of Karen's brothers introduced her to the American writer Dorothy Canfield, who loved the book and persuaded an American publisher to take it on. Karen insisted on the pen name Isak Dinesen, though it's not quite clear why. Perhaps she thought a pseudonym would give it an aura of mystery. *Seven Gothic Tales* was nominated for the Book of the Month Club and became an instant bestseller. At the age of 49 Karen Blixen was a surprise literary star.

And I think it *is* surprising that the book was so popular. The writing is hypnotically beautiful but also strange, difficult and puzzling. The stories demand careful, attentive reading. I confess that some of the tales left me utterly baffled the first time I read them. I don't just mean that I couldn't perceive the moral of the stories, I mean that I couldn't actually understand the plots. Why was the young soldier so desperate to get married? Why did the old prince challenge his young friend to a duel? I had to reread the stories and search between the lines for clues.

In 'The Monkey', a young man arrives at a convent to seek advice from his aunt, who is the Prioress. The nuns have picked up on gossip: they know he is involved in a scandal. They 'had learnt to connect it somehow with those romantic and sacred shores of ancient Greece which they had till now held in high esteem'. No doubt readers in 1934 readily understood that 'Greece' was a veiled reference to homosexuality, but it was less immediately obvious in forthright 2018. However, the opacity of the *Tales* didn't put me off. It was delicious and tantalizing. I wanted to read slowly, savouring each story and teasing it apart. When I finally interpreted the stories I felt like a detective discovering whodunnit.

Dinesen's merciful lack of plucky feminist heroines forces us to consider instead the psychology of being a woman living – and often accepting – a horribly constrained life. Sex is fraught with the dangers of childbearing and potential violence. One tale centres on an elaborately planned off-stage rape. In another, an Amazonian woman fends off a potential rapist and knocks his teeth out but later marries him. There is no happily ever after, as Dinesen's own life so amply proved.

Those women who remain spinsters have a different set of problems. In 'The Supper at Elsinore', two wealthy unmarried sisters encounter the ghost of their brother, who disappeared on the morning of his wedding many years ago and became a pirate. Since then the sisters have lived chaste, blameless lives. They attend a dinner party where the discussion turns to whether or not the guests would like to have wings. One male guest remarks that men call women angels, and they put a woman on a pedestal 'on the one inevitable condition that she must not dream of, must even have been brought up in absolute ignorance of, the possibility of flight'. They are weighed down by their cumbersome clothes, their long hair and men's 'difficult and painful laws'. Men are compared to useful prose, but women to poetry. Their sole raison d'être is to be 'lovely'.

The spinsters do not disagree. It is important to them to be lovely. Why then haven't they married? Perhaps they are doing penance for their brother's misdeeds. Perhaps no one but their brother will ever be good enough for them. Perhaps they are idealists, and 'to them the first condition of anything having real charm was this: that it must not really exist'. This being a Gothic tale, the sisters are doomed from the start. The key to their beauty is that their faces bear 'a generic resemblance to a skull'; they are destined to experience a living death. It is the two living women who are truly the ghosts in this story.

In 'The Deluge at Norderney', floodwaters sweep in around a coastal resort. While most of the holidaymakers escape, a group of three aristocrats, led by a heroic priest, swap places with four peasants trapped on the upper floor of a barn. The boatmen promise to return to collect them at dawn. By the light of a single candle, as the water rises and rises, the aristocrats spend the night drinking gin and telling their own bizarre tales. Finally the priest speaks. He reveals that he is not who he pretends to be at all; the real priest died that morning. 'I have lived long enough, by now, to have learned, when the devil grins at me, to grin back,' the imposter says. As dawn breaks the flood-water starts to lap around the characters' feet. Acting your part to perfection – and going out in style – is more important than leading a dull, honest life. Dinesen certainly lived up to that statement. She was an aristocrat and a Writer with a capital W. At the end of her life, skeletal and suffering, she put on her furs and her jewels and went on a tour of America where she socialized with Marilyn Monroe.

In the Book of the Month Club newsletter that launched *Seven Gothic Tales* into bestseller status, Dorothy Canfield wrote, 'The person who has set his teeth into a kind of fruit new to him, is usually as eager as he is unable to tell you how it tastes.' You'll have to try it yourself. So why don't you? Be brave. Grin at the devil. Take a bite.

KATE TYTE worked as an archivist for over ten years, some of them at the Royal College of Surgeons and the Natural History Museum. She now lives, teaches and writes in Lisbon.

Father Figures

MARTIN SORRELL

Three-quarters of the way through the novel I've always thought is Camus' finest, its two main protagonists go for a swim after dark in the waters beyond the harbour of their coastal city, which is in the grip of bubonic plague. The city is Oran, in north-west Algeria; the date is sometime in the 1940s. The plague, which gives the novel its name, has sealed Oran off from the outside world. The Mediterranean water into which the men plunge breathes like a fur-covered animal, Camus tells us. In it is stored the warmth of the day just ended. The two men, Dr Bernard Rieux and Jean Tarrou, both prominent in the fight against the plague, are knowingly breaking the curfew by slipping past the guards they themselves have helped set up, and heading for the sea. They're not acting out of defiance of the authorities, but to enjoy for a moment what it is they are trying to re-establish: moral and physical well-being. What, they ask as they swim alongside each other under the stars, is the point of fighting for something that can't be enjoyed?

Whenever I think of *The Plague* (1947), it's this swim that first comes to mind. It's a high point in the novel, the only moment of escape from the living entombment inside Oran. Rieux and Tarrou are powerful literary creations, fully fleshed out, complex. They're no saints, but two individuals doing their best to live by what Abraham

---

The first translation of Albert Camus' *La Peste* (1947), by Stuart Gilbert for Penguin in 1948, went unchallenged until Robin Buss produced his, also for Penguin, in 2002. It's more up-to-date, of course, and less stiff than Gilbert's: Pb · 256pp · £7.99 · ISBN 9780141185132.

Lincoln called 'the better angels of our nature'. And it's because of well-rounded characterization – of good people such as Rieux and Tarrou but also of others who can't live by Lincoln's angels, or choose not to – that I've always found *The Plague* the most rewarding of Camus' novels, the most human and the most forgiving.

I first encountered it at school. It was a set text on my French A-level syllabus. By way of preparation, our teacher – my own father, as it happened – introduced us first to Camus the man of ideas. As my father presented them, these ideas boiled down to one big one, the concept of the Absurd. To understand it was uphill work, for teacher and pupils alike. For assistance, we were pointed to two of Camus' works of non-fiction, *The Rebel* and *The Myth of Sisyphus*. I gave both a go, but still didn't understand. The next suggestion was Jean-Paul Sartre's novel *Nausea*, particularly the passage in which the protagonist Roquentin feels physically sick when the roots of a tree he's contemplating lose their identity and start to swim before his eyes in a viscous and disgusting mess; they're no longer part of the tree. In fact, *tree* no longer makes sense; the word doesn't tidy up the collection of roots, trunk, branches and leaves that's making Roquentin feel so giddy.

It was those visceral pages of *Nausea* that finally let me grasp what Camus, via my father, wanted to get into our heads, that the Absurd was about a bad relationship, like that of Roquentin with the tree, a relationship founded on a sickening irony: we humans need the world but the world doesn't need us. But – here was the uplifting next step in Camus' argument – the consequence shouldn't be despair. The Absurd didn't have to mean nihilism. The opposite in fact, because it's our human duty to rebel against it as if it *could* be overcome. And what that paradox entailed was set out nowhere more eloquently, I thought, than in Camus' plague-ridden Oran, where among the dedicated fighters of the Absurd the one who stood out was the medical doctor Bernard Rieux.

In none of the books I was studying had I encountered a figure so memorable for being so unassuming, quiet and stoical. He was the polar opposite of Meursault, the main protagonist in Camus' first and most famous novel, which my father had also suggested we read. *The Outsider* seemed to me then, and still does, just a clever game of two halves that don't fit together. Literally overnight, Meursault goes from inarticulate sensualist to eloquent philosopher. *The Outsider*, as I see it, is an awkward *roman à thèse*. So is *The Plague* – minus the awkwardness. It expands its ideas in the most unforced way. They emerge naturally from the action, as in a good play (which, in its five-part structure, *The Plague* resembles, reminding us that one of Camus' great loves was the theatre). That action and the reaction of the Oranais are shaped by the twists and turns of an unprecedented but credible medical emergency.

The situation is this. It's April 1940-something in the unremarkable coastal city of Oran, which is inhabited by unremarkable people. Camus wants us to know that these people are neither particularly virtuous nor especially contemptible. They've done nothing either to deserve what is about to descend on them or to be spared it. One ordinary day, a dead rat is found on a landing in a block of flats; then more turn up around the city. Bubonic plague has arrived, and a state of emergency is declared. The city is sealed off. No one is allowed to leave, including anyone just passing through, such as the Parisian journalist Rambert; and no one is allowed to enter, including Oranais temporarily out of town, such as Rieux's young wife, who's gone for treatment to a mountain sanatorium.

The plague claims its first human victim, then a few more, after which deaths multiply until they're so regular they seem almost normal. The authorities struggle to contain the epidemic. Prophylactic measures are tried, including a new serum. Nothing works. Religion has no answers either. The scholarly priest Father Paneloux tells his congregation that they've deserved the plague; God is punishing them for their spiritual laziness. But Paneloux begins to question God's justice and to struggle with his faith; when the plague comes to claim him, he dies clinging to his beliefs and still refusing all medical attention. The epidemic peaks in August, striking busily and randomly. Innocent young children die while unsavoury adults are spared. And then, as inexplicably as it had arrived, the plague starts to decline in the autumn, and by late January, ten months after it began, it's over. Normal life in Oran quickly resumes, but the blunt fact no one must forget is that the plague can and will descend again, anywhere, at any time. The bacillus never dies.

The story of Oran's plague year works not just as a gripping novel but also as a twofold allegory. One, of course, is of the Absurd. Oran stands for our world, in which suffering and death are indiscriminate and unjust. We could easily fall into despair, as indeed some Oranais do, notably a failed suicide called Cottard. But, Camus tells us, we can get beyond the loneliness of despair once we realize that everyone is in the same boat. *Solitaire* to *solidaire*, to use Camus' own words; from solitude to society. And no section of society fights despair more resolutely than doctors, people such as Rieux, who accept the reality of death while acting as though it can be prevented. The way Camus portrays Rieux makes him the person whom Oranais – the reader too, perhaps – can most look up to. As the novel progresses, he acquires the authority which the figure I always see as his true opposite, Father Paneloux, steadily loses.

But I've always had a more personal reason to value *The Plague*. Its other allegory – the invasion of France by Nazi Germany – connects directly with my own family's experience. My French mother's family had to endure the Occupation, some of them in their native Auvergne, others in Le Havre, most in Toulouse. So I can't help looking for parallels between them and characters in Camus' novel. My mother, for example, who had a temporary job in Bradford, couldn't go back to France, just as Rieux's wife can't return to Oran. My aunt in Toulouse, guiding Jewish friends, and once a British airman, to safe houses, reminds me of Rieux's and Tarrou's resistance to the plague; as does my grandmother, who stood up to armed men hunting a young woman they thought was inside her house – as indeed she was. As far as I know, we had no equivalents of Cottard, the black-marketeer. I like to think that in the main my French great-aunts and great-uncles and second cousins most resembled the clerk of Oran's health authority, the person Camus calls the plague's real hero, an ordinary but indomitable man who – note the significance – has been given the surname of Grand.

Imagine my shock, my parents' dismay, on hearing of Camus' death in a road accident. Around dawn on Monday, 4 January 1960 he was killed when the car in which he was being driven from Provence to Paris crashed near the Forest of Fontainebleau. He was only 46. The manner of his death had all the irony of the Absurd. He'd planned to make the overnight journey to Paris by train but was persuaded at the last moment to switch to a car. He had little time for cars, especially flashy ones such as the Facel Vega in which he met his end. People of genuine distinction, he'd told its owner, his friend and publisher Michel Gallimard, drove anonymous black Citroëns. However, the ultimate, absurd insult was to dispatch a person of such greatness so brutally, unceremoniously and in such haste.

But there was something else too, and it concerned my father. Three weeks earlier, he'd given my sixth form his final class on *The Plague*. Now, mere hours after Camus' death, he returned home from his very first day in his new job stunned by the realization that he should never have left teaching. For a while, the consequences of that departure would be disastrous. A fateful Monday indeed.

MARTIN SORRELL remembers his mother, post-war France and his father's change of career in his recent memoir, *Paulette*.

In a Class of Their Own

PATRICK WELLAND

Bored with studying, the schoolboy put aside his books and submitted to his love of writing poetry. He was aware his effort was inadequate, but he was unprepared for the verdict of an unseen witness at his shoulder. 'You shouldn't waste your sweetness on the desert air like this, Auden,' said the master who, in the way of his kind, had silkily materialized when least expected and least wanted. Years after the event at Gresham's School, a still furious WH wrote: 'Today, I cannot think of him without wishing him evil.'

This entertaining vignette, typifying the world-weary teacher confronted by the apparently idle enthusiasms of youth – and made more amusing by the identity of the victim – is recalled in *The Old School*, a collection of classroom memories edited by Graham Greene and published in 1934 when he was 30.

Few experiences remain so solidly imprinted on the mind as those of school. Youthful friends and enemies tend to be remembered for life, along with ancient episodes of teasing and bullying, indiscipline and eccentricity. To this day I cannot recall without a shudder dismal winter afternoons spent in fruitless quest of a soggy ball. I am still amazed at the sheer sadism of a teacher whose brutally enthusiastic use of the cane would today have him in the dock. And the memory of a Latin teacher, baited beyond endurance, bringing down on the head of his young tormentor a weighty classical dictionary, thereby inducing moderate concussion, lives with me still. Yet though school

---

Graham Greene (ed.), *The Old School: Essays by Divers Hands* (1934), is out of print.

dominates childhood it often makes only a brief appearance in biography or autobiography. This is a pity. The dramas of school may in themselves be minor, but in their variety of experience they provide a fertile soil of recollection.

The Old School is made up of seventeen essays by writers who achieved literary distinction later in life, though some are all but forgotten today. Apart from Auden, still familiar names include Harold Nicolson, H. E. Bates, Anthony Powell, Elizabeth Bowen and Stephen Spender. Less well remembered are the South African novelist and poet William Plomer and the novelist and film critic E. Arnot Robertson.

The bulk of them deal with grammar or public-school life in the years shortly before, during and immediately after the First World War. Here we have L. P. Hartley looking back with amused toler-ance on the stultified absurdities of Harrow, Harold Nicolson still 'gnashing my teeth' at being unjustly accused of cheating at Wellington and the publisher and poet Derek Verschoyle railing at the 'paralysing uniformity' of Malvern. Here too are memories of a less privileged world. Sean O'Faolain remembers his school outside Cork where 'every second boy was barelegged, with the mud drying between his toes and zoomorphic tracery on his shins from sitting in the ashes of his laneway home'. Walter Greenwood recalls with horror his Langworthy Road council school in Salford, an establishment in seemingly permanent revolt where 'the teachers' disgust for us was only equalled by our disgust for them, and for the school'.

Though writing only twenty years after the outbreak of the Great War, Greene is aware that these are reports from a vanishing age. In his preface, he predicts that 'the system which this book mainly represents, is doomed' and describes the collection as a 'premature memorial . . . like a gathering of the staid and unloved hovering, in the most absurd headgear, unconsciously upon the "brink"'.

He is right, of course. The colonial attitudes that underpinned the pre-war public-school system have long vanished. But the triumphs and defeats, joys and miseries of any school life are timeless. Hartley (Harrow, b. 1895) entitles his essay 'The Conformer', suggesting he was happy with a regime which treated individual eccentricity with tolerance but frowned on any challenge to tradition. Offenders were frequently punished by a beating from older boys, leading to the occasional 'mild epidemic of flagellation'. Hartley, who claims at the time of writing to be a timorous adult who cannot even utter a rebuke, admits: 'As Head of House I did not shrink from summoning my subjects to my room, telling them how awful they were and what a thankless and distasteful job it was to have their welfare in my charge; nor did I mind "whopping" delinquents and I occasionally took practice shots against the curtain of my bed to get my hand in.'

Anthony Powell (*bottom left*) at Eton, *c.* 1919

Anthony Powell (Eton, b. 1905) languidly admits that he spent his entire school career in 'well deserved obscurity', in his leisure time beagling, going to Tap – the drinking room reserved for the College's senior boys – playing poker, indulging in the occasional Russian cigarette and 'brooding on romantic agitations of the moment which seem in retrospect so extravagant'. It was assumed by the staff that every boy would at some future time be in some such exalted position as Viceroy of India and was therefore taught accordingly. This, he says, might produce anything from 'industrious civil servants to megalomaniac noblemen'.

The Great War looms darkly over this apparently settled world and is vividly recalled by William Plomer (Rugby, b. 1903). He remembers that while studying at his 'sour and ugly' prep school, the windows would be rattled by the 'interminable thunder' of the guns in Flanders. In the school holidays, he watched errand boys in khaki being taught by a sergeant to stab straw-filled sacks painted with the likeness of the Kaiser. Moving to Rugby, he found that the attrition on the Western Front was reflected in the competence of his teachers. So many men were serving abroad that those schoolmasters left were 'either dotards or weaklings' marked by sadism and lack of warmth, imagination and culture.

H. E. Bates (Kettering Grammar, b. 1905) waspishly remembers being 'suckled at the vinegary breasts of repressed and impossible mistresses'. He is rescued from unhappiness by the arrival in 1919 of a young teacher whose 'quiet and almost melancholy understanding' transformed his schooldays and set him on the road to a literary life. Poignantly, the teacher had returned from the front 'without several of his fingers and with his face atrociously mutilated and his legs and arms stiff from wounds'.

The girls have other worrying matters on their minds. The future novelist Theodora Benson (Cheltenham Ladies' College, b. 1906) says: 'I believe that hardly anyone knew what are so exclusively called THE facts of life . . . one of the girls asked me once how babies came. I had a sort of hazy idea but was not very sure of my ground, so I benevolently answered that I thought I should only embarrass both of us by telling her.' With boys and the regrettable temptations they represent safely absent, passions are channelled into calf love between the girls. 'Amazed and disgusted' at such behaviour, robust Theodora remembers one victim telling her: 'It's so heartless to like Patsy better than me, when you think how I filled her hot water bottle for every night of the winter term. I don't think Patsy would have filled her hot water bottle for her every night – at least I'm sure she wouldn't have done it in quite the same way.'

The novelist Eileen Arnot Robertson (Sherborne, b. 1903) observes that an English public school for girls was run on a male system imperfectly adapted for female needs – 'run about, girls, like boys, and then you won't think of them! Boys . . . horrid with three stars in the Baedeker of the Nasty which ruled our young lives'. Her peers were the 'most thoroughgoing prigs imaginable' who skipped through their schooldays with the 'slightly hysterical' attitude of 'Oh, goody-goody-we-ought-to-do-well-in-lacrosse-this-term. Hurrah-for-the-house-and-I'm-so-glad-I'm-not-pretty!' She was determined not to conform, most dramatically by refusing to be confirmed. This was so alarming that two prefects walked her round the grounds trying to change her mind. As the best reason they could find in favour of confirmation was that the preparation was 'simply topping' and religion was 'so sensible', it is hardly surprising that their seduction techniques failed. Eileen, whose abundant good humour and common sense shine through her prose, went on to become a regular on the humorous radio show *My Word!*

Disenchanted Derek Verschoyle (Malvern, b. 1911) displays an acid contempt worthy of John Osborne as he heaps abuse on the public-school system. At best, he concludes, it will produce a practical and tolerant man. At worst, the product is a 'complacent philistine, unable to think for himself . . . lacking in imagination and vision, eager for popularity, emotionally dwarfed and blandly adolescent in sexual matters, insensitive to beauty and confused towards truth'. And so the rant goes on. It is no surprise to learn that Verschoyle, literary editor of the *Spectator* between 1932 and 1939, is remembered in the '50s by Diana Athill as a 'raffish figure' given to shooting cats with his .22 rifle while lolling before his window with feet on desk.

One of the joys of this collection is that we see some of the most talented writers of their generation flexing their early literary muscles. An exception is Harold Nicolson (Wellington, b. 1886) who at the time of writing was in his late forties. Age did not dampen his outrage that his essay 'upon a piece of coal' thirty years earlier was considered to be the worst in class. With not a trace of irony, he complains: 'I presumed that what was required was not so much a discourse upon the Industrial Revolution as an examination of the responses and associations evoked by the contemplation of coal in detail.' Yet ultimately Nicolson is forgiving of his alma mater. In a lovely phrase, he says of a visit he made to the school as an adult: 'There was a faint breeze in the air from the olives of Academe; the old pine-laden heartiness had lost its cruel tang.'

And so to Greene himself, who provides the last word with memories of Berkhamsted, where his father was head. 'It was not a really satisfactory school for sadists,' he says. 'Only two sadistic masters come back to mind, and one of them was so openly sadistic, so cheerful a debauchee, that one could not grudge him his pleasure.' But Greene is disenchanted by the Old School in general, denouncing its excessive code of sexual purity, its rules designed only for the convenience of the authorities and its distrustful attitude that privacy can only be misused. Instead he puts his hopes for the future in the State school, seeing it as an extension of the old village school. He says: 'It is at least better that he [the pupil] should learn loyalty to a town which includes all classes and both sexes than to an institution consisting only of his own sex and own class.'

This was 1934 and both public and state schools have since changed in ways Greene and his contributors could never have imagined. But, dated as they are, these recollections reflect at heart the same youthful intensities experienced by today's so much savvier pupils. Everyone has a story about their schooldays: if only they were all so well recounted.

PATRICK WELLAND remembers his B-team public school set in disagreeable countryside with little affection, but he is grateful to it for instilling an enduring dislike of organized activities.

Front Lines

SUE GAISFORD

There were four of us gathered at Mr Morgan's grave, one icy morning in January 1978. I held my newborn son close, as the sleet-laden wind sliced across the vast west London cemetery. The brief ceremony ended, we turned to leave. The matron of Mr Morgan's nursing-home remarked that no next-of-kin had been found, and I asked her what would happen to his things. She gave me a sharp look, saying there was nothing but a filthy old envelope he had seemed to cherish: I could have it, if I wanted.

In fact it was all I wanted. A neighbour of ours, Mr Morgan had become a firm friend, and the document in that envelope was the source of his greatest pride. I knew it by heart. Delivered towards the end of May 1915, it is addressed to his parents in Pontypridd. It informs them that their son William, of the Welch Regiment, had died at L'Epinette on 9 May 1915. Included with this is a neatly typed note: 'The King commands me to assure you of the true sympathy of His Majesty and The Queen in your sorrow.' The big, bold, black signature reads 'Kitchener'. Of course it wasn't true.

It is, however, a printed record of (a part of) Mr Morgan's service in the trenches. A wily young Welsh lad, he'd joined up in 1914 as a private soldier, which position he managed, on and off, to retain throughout the hostilities. Raymond Asquith, roughly fifteen years his senior, joined later, moving straight into the officer class: he left a

H. H. Asquith, *Letters to Venetia Stanley* · eds. Michael and Eleanor Brock (OUP, 1982) and Raymond Asquith, *Life and Letters* · ed. John Jolliffe (Collins, 1980) are both out of print but we can obtain second-hand copies.

record of extraordinary cool courage, and some powerfully moving letters, edited and selected by his grandson. And Raymond's father, born 26 years earlier still in 1878, had become Prime Minister by the time the Morgan parents received the dreaded telegram. His own, published letters are the most surprising of the war.

When the telegram boy knocked at the Morgans' door, their son William was in fact hiding upstairs. After enduring hours of incessant shelling during the Battle of Aubers Ridge, he had regained consciousness in a dark, blunted and smouldering forest near Festubert, surrounded by dead comrades. Noticing that two fingers of his left hand were now missing, he decided that he'd had enough. I wish I knew how he managed it but, somehow or other, he made his way back to Wales, buried his uniform in his parents' garden, and lay low.

Had they caught him in France, he would have been shot. As it was, a neighbour alerted the Military Police and he served a spell in the comparative comfort of Reading Gaol, before being returned to his regiment to fight (and survive) many another day. In old age, his attitude to the whole thing was sublimely jaunty and devil-may-care, the stories he told full of sauciness and misadventure, a million miles from any official records. Now only the telegram survives, fragile, torn and filthy but still legible, wrapped in greasy brown paper. Included with it is a note about claiming his effects, if effects there should prove to be. Unusually, there is no personal letter from his commanding officer.

It is scarcely surprising. On 9 May 1915, the British Army sustained 11,000 casualties, one of the highest rates of daily loss during that entire appalling war. Those officers who survived could scarcely have been expected to write, immediately, in detail, about every one of the men (presumed) lost in that one day.

But they probably did. Perhaps, a little later, someone even started to write to William Morgan's parents, before realizing the truth. It was an unavoidable duty to write in consolation to the next-of-kin of every man fallen and, though the classic line was that he died a hero, killed instantly in the heat of battle, that was very seldom even part of the true story. However, when the surviving officer had known the dead soldiers well, these letters are their most eloquent obituaries.

Letters supported and sustained everyone a century ago. The postal service was never better, and people wrote as often as today they tweet, certain that their letters would be delivered within a few hours. The Prime Minister, H. H. Asquith, was married to the formidable Margot, but he fell in love with Venetia Stanley. More a serial romantic than a philanderer, he wrote her an astonishing 560 letters between 1912 and 1915, up to four times a day, stopping only when she became engaged to Edwin Montagu. These letters present a fascinating, sidelong view of the government and the characters who peopled it. He wrote to her during Cabinet meetings, at the worst crises of the war; he wrote frequently, lengthily, devotedly.

At the time of Mr Morgan's unscheduled departure from the Western Front, for example, on a calamitous day described by Vera Brittain as 'the sort of day that made one begin to wonder if it was possible for the world to continue', a day culminating in the news that the RMS *Lusitania* had been torpedoed off the Old Head of Kinsale with the loss of 1,198 lives, Asquith was writing to Venetia about a 'rather straggling' kind of Cabinet; about Mr Selfridge coming to lunch; about distracting himself with rereading *Measure for Measure*; and about the American President who'd been 'making a speech . . . to "Americans of alien birth" stuffed with even more than the usual allowance of swollen and sterile platitudes'. That was President Wilson, of course.

The Prime Minister was blazingly indiscreet, prefacing the most vital secrets of military strategy with such remarks as 'this is rather private' and reminding her not to leave the letter lying on the hall table. And his thumbnail sketches of his colleagues are wickedly enjoyable: arguing with Churchill, he wrote, was like arguing with a brass band, but even that was preferable to listening to his eloquence.

He heard with chill despair Winston declare that the last thing he'd pray for was peace: 'having tasted blood, he is beginning, like a tiger, to raven for more'.

But Asquith did not write to his son. In the course of that war, the British Army Postal Service delivered around 2 billion letters to the troops. In one year alone, more than 19,000 mailbags crossed the Channel every day, delivering post to soldiers on the Western Front, following them in and out of the front line, support trenches and rest billets, always and remarkably getting through. Yet, as Raymond Asquith wrote to his wife Katherine on 22 August 1916, 'during my ten months' exile here the PM has never written me a line, of any description'.

He must have regretted it. Raymond was his eldest son, the first child of his marriage to Helen Melland, who had died in 1891 when Raymond was 12. The bright, sensitive boy felt his mother's loss keenly all his life, as he admitted years later to H. T. Baker, his best friend, and the recipient of many of his letters. Nevertheless, he was to achieve, via Winchester and Oxford, very nearly every possible academic triumph, save only one. As he wrote to his father, his entry came only *proxime* (second) in the 1900 Gaisford Prize for Greek Verse, which Baker had won outright the previous year. Typically, languidly, he explains: 'as most of mine was written in a cab driving to Aberlady, I couldn't expect anything else'.

That elegant languor characterizes many of his early letters, mostly written during the famously long, idle, flannelled and fancifully aphoristic sunset of the Edwardian age. 'Nothing', he wrote to his father from Balliol, 'disgusts the average Englishman so much as to see his own methods adopted by another nation', adding, soon afterwards, 'I enclose my tailor's bill for the year, which I hold to be moderate.' Little wonder that his grandson, introducing a selection of Raymond's extraordinary letters, remarks that the years he lived 'sometimes seem as remote from the present as the Middle Ages'.

His vocabulary was replete with words such as apolaustic and banausic, about which he would bombinate, but he could also be very funny: his parody of Kipling, beginning 'The sun, like a bishop's bottom/ Rosy and round and hot . . .' doesn't bear reproducing here in full, but is unforgettable, as is his comment on Alfred Douglas's heart-rending lines about the imprisonment of Oscar Wilde. This is the verse:

> Alas I have lost my God
> My beautiful God Apollo
> Wherever his footsteps trod
> My feet were wont to follow.

There is 'just a reminiscence', writes Raymond, 'of Mary had a little lamb . . . which adds a certain piquancy of contrast'.

But when he fell in love and, later, when he went to war, the scherzo gave way to a graver and mightier rhythm. His early love-letters to Katherine Horner, whose 'eyes could draw a limpet from a rock and deaden the conscience of an archangel', are as elaborate and as yearningly gorgeous as Keats's. God, he suggests to her, has taken '400 years working steadily, with many failures . . . to produce at last in flesh the divine type which Botticelli conceived but could never quite express'.

They were married in 1907, and his letters thereafter are evidence of a growing and deepening mutual trust. Many soldiers, of all ranks, chose to spare their families the real horrors of the trenches, but Raymond did not. He tells Katherine of picking over the ruins of Sanctuary Wood: 'nothing but twisted and blackened stumps and a mesh of shell-holes, dimpling into one another, full of mud and blood, and dead men and over-fed rats which blundered into one in the twilight like fat moths'. Later, he fears that one of the chief effects of war 'is to make one more callous, short-sighted and unimaginative than one is by nature'.

By nature he was none of those things. His was a haunting and profound intelligence, his name a byword for cool courage and commitment, tempered with compassion and characterized by unshakeable integrity. No easy Christian comforts for him on the battlefield: he wrote that he despised those religious people who called themselves worms and were then furious when God did not treat them as emperors. On the death of a dear friend he writes, 'A blind God butts about the world with a pair of delicately malignant antennae to detect whatever is fit to live and an iron hoof to stamp it into the dust.' His own turn came on 15 September 1916. Shot in the chest during the Battle of Flers-Courcelette, he casually lit a cigarette so that his men would not be disheartened. He died on the stretcher shortly afterwards.

A hundred years on, the Great War continues to fascinate and appal. It is a unique phenomenon, capable of being seen or interpreted in innumerable ways. As literary editors know, scarcely a week goes by without another book appearing, always apparently taking a new approach. However, even in such a crowded auditorium, the Asquiths' letters deserve a fairer hearing than most, informed, frank, intimate and unfiltered as they are, and written, they believed privately, to the women they trusted and loved.

But truth is an elusive chimera. Soon after Mr Morgan first showed me his mendacious telegram, I returned from his battlefields and told him about seeing the British cemeteries with their poignant lines of tombstones, each inscribed with the name of some young soldier.

As always, he was ready to surprise me. 'Oh, you don't want to believe a word of that,' he said, dismissively: 'I put three dead Germans in most of those graves myself.'

SUE GAISFORD began reviewing books for *The Economist* about the time of Mr Morgan's death, and has since written for many other publications. She currently reviews for the *Financial Times* and is on the judging panel for the annual Authors' Club Best First Novel Award.

Moscow under the Terror

MICHAEL BARBER

In ancient days, whenever I was in Richmond-upon-Thames, I would walk up the hill to the Baldur Bookshop where, if you succeeded in running the gauntlet of its cantankerous owner, John Barton, there was nearly always something that was worth the hike. That said, I can't imagine why I bought a tourist's guide to the city of Moscow, published in 1937. Was it because its previous owner was a Mrs C. J. Webb, suggesting some connection with those 'useful idiots', Beatrice and Sydney? ('We are ikons in the Soviet Union,' boasted Beatrice.) Whatever the reason it certainly wasn't because I immediately grasped the baleful significance of such a guide to such a place at such a time.

Written by the Co-operative Publishing Society of Foreign Workers in the USSR, the guide describes Moscow as 'the city of emancipated and joyful labour'. In fact it was a huge building site over which hovered the angel of death. The architect of this apoca-lyptic landscape was Josef Stalin, who had promised Muscovites that in future life would become 'merrier'. In 1935 he approved a ten-year plan that would do for Moscow what Haussmann had done for nine-teenth-century Paris. But unlike Haussmann, Stalin could knock down any building he liked (conservationists protested at their peril). He could also call upon an inexhaustible supply of forced labour,

---

The Co-operative Publishing Society of Foreign Workers in the USSR, *Guide to the City of Moscow: A Handbook for Tourists, with Information on the City's Past, Present and Future, Descriptions of its Museums and Points of Interest* (1937), is now a collector's item, with copies for sale on eBay and AbeBooks at upwards of US$200. A copy is available in the London Library.

described in the guide as 'criminals undergoing rehabilitation' – thousands of whom had already died in the construction of such projects as the White Sea–Baltic Canal and the Moscow–Volga Canal.

That Moscow was in need of a makeover was indisputable. In 1934, on his first visit there, Guy Burgess described it as 'just a Balkan town – you know, pigs in the trams'. The streets teemed with peasants who had been driven off the land by collectivization and ensuing famine. They found jobs – unemployment did not exist in the Soviet Union – but so ramshackle was the infrastructure that for most of the city's 5 million inhabitants everyday life was a constant struggle. While acknowledging that there could be no new social order without a modern infrastructure, Stalin's blueprint gave pride of place to the Palace of the Soviets, a monolithic 'wedding cake' over 400 metres high and surmounted by a 100-metre high statue of Lenin. Work on this enormous folly was halted by the Nazi invasion and the site eventually became an open-air swimming-pool. Today the huge cathedral that Stalin demolished to make way for the Palace has been rebuilt.

A year after the plan was approved Moscow became the epicentre of an even more cataclysmic event, the great purge of Party members that would result in 700,000 deaths and imprisonment in the Gulag for 2 million more. The purge was known as the Yezhovshchina, a reference to Stalin's hated police chief Nikolai Yezhov, who, like his predecessor Yagoda, was later shot. The Yezhovshchina reached its climax in 1937. It is recalled in Vasily Grossman's epic novel, *Life and Fate* (see *SF* no. 16), by one of the protagonists: 'It had been especially terrible to walk down Komsomolsky Alley and Lubyanka Street during the summer nights of

1937 . . . The whole city seemed to be pinned down, fascinated by the glassy stare of the Lubyanka.'

In the guide the Lubyanka is disguised by its bland official title, the People's Commissariat of Internal Affairs. Naturally no mention is made of how busy it has suddenly become, but on p. 79 we learn that a nearby street has been renamed in memory of S. M. Kirov, 'one of the most beloved leaders of the working class who was treacherously murdered by counter-revolutionary terrorists in 1934 in Leningrad'. It's now accepted that Stalin connived at the murder of Kirov, whom he saw as a potential rival, and then used it as a pretext to launch the purge.

Nikita Khrushchev, later to denounce Stalin but in the 1930s his zealous subordinate, is supposed to have overheard his boss mutter, 'I trust no one, not even myself.' There was no antidote to his toxic mixture of paranoia and megalomania. After weeks of softening up followed by a cleverly stage-managed show trial at which they confessed to extraordinary crimes, his victims were summarily dispatched by a single shot to the back of the head. The overworked executioners were supplied with unlimited vodka and buckets of eau de cologne – to mask the reek of gunpowder and blood. Even dogs, it was said, shrank from them in terror.

The 'counter-revolutionary terrorists' who supposedly murdered Kirov are identified in the guide as Trotskyites, a term that was also synonymous with 'spies', 'saboteurs', 'double-dealers' and 'wreckers'. Although in exile, Trotsky was regarded as Public Enemy Number One, the villain responsible for just about everything that went wrong in the world's first socialist state. And yet that state would never have existed without Trotsky, the creator and motivator of the Red Army, which probably explains why so many of the top brass were eliminated in the purge. For readers of the guide, he is the elephant in the room. The civil war was won without him, and it is Lenin and Stalin who sit above the salt in the Red Army Museum.

When I first looked through the guide I assumed only fellow

travellers would have had a use for it. Who but a Soviet sympathizer would traipse round such spectacles as the Museum of Bolsheviks in Tsarist Penal Servitude and Exile? Then I learnt that the writer Anthony Powell, a staunch Tory, had gone to Moscow in 1936. What drew him was the Museum of Modern Western Art, which housed, he thought, the finest collection of French Impressionist and Post-Impressionist art in the world. Powell had Lenin to thank for this. Instead of selling off the paintings, acquired by two canny Tsarist collectors, in 1918 he nationalized them, 'having regard for their usefulness in educating the people'. Powell was lucky he went when he did. In 1939 Stalin shut down the museum and later dispersed its contents on the grounds that they were 'devoid of any progressive civilizing worth'.

Had you taken Walk 14 in the guide you would have passed the House on the Embankment, a huge apartment block reminiscent of London's Dolphin Square, which faced the Kremlin across the Moscow River. Reserved for the party élite, this address had a rapid turnover of tenants during the purge. Whole families disappeared overnight, their absence referred to obliquely: 'They've gone on a journey. We don't know when they'll be back.' But high-profile arrests sometimes took place in public, and this was the fate of those responsible for overseeing the construction of the Moscow–Volga Canal, described by the guide as 'the greatest undertaking of its kind in the world'. On the day of its official opening, 15 July 1937, witnesses saw several of these unlucky men being hauled off a boat and driven away under guard.

The guide reminds tourists that they enjoy 'special privileges' in the Soviet Union, including access to shops selling luxuries no ordinary Soviet citizen could afford (this, of course, is left unsaid). By way of a little light reading it recommends some classics of Marxism-Leninism, including a recently published work of Stalin's called *Defects in Party Work and Measures for Liquidating Trotskyite and Other Double-Dealers*. Paradoxically, this pamphlet probably saved the lives of George Orwell and his wife. As he recounts in *Homage to Catalonia*, the Spanish government's secret police, conducting their own purge of heretics who included the Workers' Party of Marxist Unification militia in which Orwell had served, were 'reassured' to discover a copy of the pamphlet when searching the Orwells' hotel bedroom in Barcelona.

The Spanish Civil War came at an opportune moment for Stalin, whose excesses had alienated prominent Popular Front supporters like André Gide and Edmund Wilson. In return for most of the Spanish government's gold reserves, he sent just enough men and matériel to ensure that Madrid held out against Franco and his Fascist allies. This steadied the ship. As Arthur Koestler put it: 'When the first Russian fighters appeared in the skies of battered Madrid all of us who had lived through the agony of the defenceless town felt that they were the saviours of civilization.' But Koestler soon became disillusioned. Like Orwell he realized that Stalin's henchmen in Spain were more concerned to purge deviationists than prosecute the war. In 1940 he wrote *Darkness at Noon*, in which an old Bolshevik is persuaded to confess to crimes he didn't commit 'for the sake of the Party'. It remains the definitive fictional indictment of Stalinism.

But as Stalin had predicted, most Western liberals, mesmerized by the threat of Fascism, did swallow his version of events, however implausible. Hence, presumably, this flippant line from the Hollywood comedy romance *Ninotchka*, starring Greta Garbo, which was released in October 1939. Playing a poker-faced Soviet trade official on a mission to Paris, Garbo is met at the station by some of her colleagues. 'How is Moscow?' they ask. 'Very good,' she answers. 'The last mass trials were a great success. There are going to be fewer – but better – Russians.'

MICHAEL BARBER writes regularly for *Slightly Foxed* and *The Oldie*. He has never been to Moscow.

Trips to the Past

SOPHIE BREESE

When I was 7 I was sent to stay with my grandparents in the seaside town of Broadstairs, where I was seen and not heard, learned good table manners and pretended I was a landlocked mermaid. I also read books, for what else can an imaginative little girl do when television is forbidden and conversations rarely take account of her age?

My grandmother was not a reader and so there were few books in the house, just some nineteenth-century novels which had belonged to her mother, and a single shelf of books in a glass-fronted cabinet containing *The Country Diary of an Edwardian Lady*, coffee-table books about the Yorkshire Dales, the Lakes and Cornwall, and Daphne du Maurier's *The House on the Strand*. I fell on the latter, and I have read it many times since.

Set in Cornwall, it is a brilliantly compelling story told in recognizable du Maurier style: civil disturbance lurks in the background; it has a frustratingly passive narrator; and it deals with that all too painful subject, unrequited love. But whereas some of her novels hint at the supernatural, this one is a true time-travel story.

Dick Young is staying in Kilmarth, the large Cornish house of his eccentric friend from Cambridge days, the scientist Magnus Lane. Ostensibly using the holiday to decide whether or not to take a publishing job in the United States, Dick seems actually to be in escape mode, running from a tricky marriage and from his future. A more profound escape is offered him in the form of some experimental

Daphne du Maurier, *The House on the Strand* (1969)
Virago · Pb · 352pp · £8.99 · ISBN 9781844080427

potions Magnus has been brewing in what he calls 'Bluebeard's Chamber'. One dose and Dick finds himself standing in exactly the same building, but 650 years earlier. Shadowing an apparent alter ego Roger Kylmerth, he observes the noble families of that period, their love affairs, their betrayals, their political choices and, in several cases, their deaths. But Dick can do nothing to intervene: if he so much as touches one of these apparitions, he is propelled violently back to his own time with disturbing side effects that include nausea and episodes of paralysis.

Over the next few weeks Dick takes several trips back into the past, and 'trips' is the right word. This novel, one of du Maurier's last, appeared in 1969, and later in the story the secret potion is compared by a doctor to LSD. Dick, however, believes he is actually living the experiences through Roger. Magnus, most of the time at the end of a phone, tells Dick that he too has had these experiences and encountered the same people. For the reader, or at least for me, it doesn't really matter how Dick gets back to the early fourteenth century. I found I was more interested in his increasing displacement from his present-day life and was impatient for him to leave the nagging of his unpleasant-sounding wife and disappear into medieval Cornwall.

Dick's 'other world' as he calls it is not a safe retreat, however, but a place of constant danger, full of disease, murder and political intrigue. Because Roger, Dick's guide, is steward to Sir Henry and Lady Joanna Champernoune, it is their story that Dick initially follows until he finds himself getting to know members of the extended family, including Sir Otto Bodrugan and his lover Isolda. Both Dick and Roger become obsessed with this affair: we witness Otto and Isolda's secret meetings and their inevitable tragic end.

Gradually Dick becomes unable to distinguish between the two worlds, finding that back in the 1960s he starts talking about events from the faraway past as if they had happened only moments ago. The dangers of the drug become clearer as Dick, like both Roger and Otto, falls in love with Isolda; Magnus dies in a particularly violent way while on a visit to fourteenth-century Cornwall; and Dick nearly kills his own wife, thinking she is someone from the past. Dick is an unpleasant man in many ways – selfish and misogynistic, refusing to take responsibility for his own life – but it is a testament to du Maurier's writing that one is able to sympathize with him.

Back in modern-day Cornwall, Dick begins to explore the reality of his visions. He tracks down family records in the local library; he finds evidence of births in the church records; and he wanders through the twentieth-century Cornish landscape, using an Ordnance Survey map to link present-day buildings with those of the past. He is particularly fascinated by the story of Kilmarth/Kylmerth, the house in which he is staying, which was, it turns out, his alter ego's home centuries ago.

Dick's interest in the building echoes that of du Maurier herself. The novel is set in the house in which by 1969 she was actually living, and she too explored the local records and maps to create a story with a basis in historical fact. Two years earlier Philip Rashleigh, the owner of the house called Menabilly which du Maurier had rented for twenty-five years, had decided he would not renew her lease, and had suggested she move to the dower house, known by then as Kilmarth. An early inspection of Kilmarth showed her that a previous tenant had been a professor who kept animal embryos in the basement, the source perhaps for the character of Magnus; she also discovered that the foundations of the house dated back to 1329 and that various members of the local gentry had been involved in a plot against Edward III; all the families described in the past of the novel were real, as was Roger Kylmerth. At the end of the novel, du Maurier shows the reader evidence of her own research, including a map of the local area linking past and present, plus a (real) family tree of the key players.

The House on the Strand is not the only du Maurier novel to feature a house and its secrets in such an important way: Menabilly provided the setting for both *Rebecca* (as Manderley) and *The King's General*. In all three novels, the buildings are presented as storehouses of memories, not just for the people alive at that moment but also for those who have once occupied them. The ghost of Rebecca can only truly be laid to rest once Manderley is burnt down.

A few years after writing *The House on the Strand*, du Maurier gathered together her early diaries in *Myself When Young*. In them she explains her fascination with the buildings in which she lived:

> Who can ever affirm, or deny that the houses which have sheltered us as children, or as adults, and our predecessors too, do not have embedded in their walls, one with the dust and cobwebs, one with the overlay of fresh wallpaper and paint, the imprint of what-has-been, the suffering, the joy? We are all ghosts of yesterday, and the phantom of tomorrow awaits us alike in sunshine or in shadow, dimly perceived at times, never entirely lost.

These words also make me realize why the novel has exercised such a hold on me. It is inextricably linked to my three-month stay with my grandparents: when I read *The House on the Strand* now I find myself simultaneously in du Maurier's Cornwall, past and present, and in Grandma and Grandpa's house on Westcliff Road, Broadstairs, in the 1970s.

Once my grandparents had died I didn't return to Broadstairs for many years. When, suddenly wanting to explore my own past, I did go back, the sense of *déjà vu* that Dick describes so well – those echoes across time of memories in landscape and in buildings – made sense to me. Grandma's front door, no longer green, was open as I approached the house, so naturally I went in. Removal men were in the process of emptying the place, so I took advantage of the chaos to look around. Like Dick, I was in my own present, my own past and the imagined past of the previous hundred years when the house had first been owned by our family: some walls had been knocked down and the garden was a different shape, but the memories were still there. For a brief moment it seemed that nothing had changed and that Grandma was sitting in her chair, passing me her copy of *The House on the Strand* and telling me to take good care of it.

SOPHIE BREESE continues to be fascinated by ghosts and is currently tracing the story of her French parents-in-law's thick-walled medieval house in a village in the Dordogne.

A Well-tempered Gardener

MICHAEL LEAPMAN

There is no good reason why an expert and dedicated gardener should be able to write elegant prose – and a survey of the gardening shelves of bookshops, along with the many magazines devoted to horticulture, will confirm that the two skills rarely converge. One glittering exception was Christopher Lloyd, known familiarly as Christo, who died in 2006 havebaying spent almost his entire adult life developing the five-acre garden at Great Dixter, his family home in East Sussex, where he was born in 1921. He wrote columns about it for *Country Life* and other journals, and produced seventeen books.

Although he was deadly serious about gardening, his writing was always unstuffy, telling us almost as much about him and his acquaintances as about his plants and preferences. He would use the reactions of others to clarify his own ideas. The very first sentence of his best-known book, *The Well-Tempered Garden* – originally published in 1970 and revised and reprinted many times since – hints at this: 'Friends sometimes ask me to deliver post mortems on their less successful gardening efforts, but it is very difficult to pronounce with any certainty when their case history has been thoroughly masked.' This slightly irritable tone, bordering on the curmudgeonly, per-

Christopher Lloyd, *The Well-Tempered Garden* (1970) • Weidenfeld & Nicolson • Pb • 384pp • £16.99 • ISBN 9781780227825; *In My Garden: The Garden Diaries of Great Dixter* (1993) • Bloomsbury • Pb • 288pp • £10.99 • ISBN 9781408811085. His *Cuttings* (2007) is out of print but we can obtain second-hand copies.

meates much of his writing, and is part of what makes it fun to read.

The Well-Tempered Garden is today recognized as a classic of the genre; yet the essence of Christo's approach is more sharply delineated in his numerous columns. He wrote for *Country Life* unfailingly every week from 1962 until 2005: a selection was published in 1993 under the title *In My Garden*. In 1989 he began a column for the *Guardian* which continued until shortly before he died. Some of these were collected in *Cuttings* in 2007.

As it happens, 1993 was also the year when I first became acquainted with him, both through his writing and in person. He had been born into gardening; my own belated introduction to the craft was very different. In 1974 I was editor of the diary column in *The Times*. It was the year of the long miners' strike, resulting in power cuts and, briefly, the three-day working week. All that brought on a general feeling that we were approaching the end of civilization as we knew it. Self-sufficiency became the watchword and there was a sudden surge in demand for allotments. To test how hard it was to acquire one I put in applications to several bodies and wrote a diary item about their discouraging responses – then forgot all about it.

A year later I received a letter from the Thames Water Authority inviting me to take over an allotment outside their Brixton waterworks. I decided to take the plunge, so that I could write occasional diary items on the travails of a novice gardener. These quickly caught the imagination of readers, who sent me letters of encouragement and advice, as well as seeds and cuttings. I was even persuaded to write a book about it (*One Man and His Plot*, 1976). As a result, before long I was approached by editors to write about gardens – as a reporter, never an expert – adding an extra string to my journalistic bow.

Because it all started with the allotment, my prime horticultural interest has always been fruit and vegetables. Although Christo did grow them – and was by all accounts an excellent cook – they were clearly secondary to his principal passion for plants. In *The Well-Tempered Garden*, he devotes only sixteen pages to the kitchen garden, at the very end of the book. The chapter starts in characteristically combative style, with the author quarrelling with his brother about whether it is worth growing vegetables at all. His brother seeks to goad him: 'The difference between this cabbage and what I should buy at Bristol is that there's twice as much waste on what you have grown.'

'I could not argue,' Christo writes.

It was only too obviously true. The slugs had made deep inroads. In fact our cabbages get picked with the slugs inside them, and if not dealt with for a few days the slugs emerge and are found at night crawling around the kitchen draining board. However, when he saw our leeks, my brother did exclaim that they looked nice. He made no comparisons this time but I knew that he had in mind the market article, more than half of which consists of green leaves with only a very short, blanched stump. In a garden you can do the job properly, taking out a trench wide enough to plant a double row and then earthing them up to get a really long white stem.

See how he camouflages sound technical advice within a punchy personal anecdote.

He was never averse to challenging received opinion, and in April 1993 hit the headlines by announcing in *Country Life* that he was going to uproot nearly all the roses from his historic rose garden – designed in 1912 by the architect Edwin Lutyens – and replace them with lush tropical-style plants. 'Seeing that the soil is excellent for any other plant except for the rose, which has fouled its own patch,' he wrote, 'I do not see why I should be made a slave to this one flower, which occupies no greater a place in my affections than many another.' Some critics were horrified, pointing out that a bed of roses has long been seen as an essential component of the traditional English garden. Would its abandonment by one of the nation's leading plantsmen lead to its eventual demise?

In the wake of this controversy I was asked by the magazine *Gardens Illustrated* to interview the great man. I did so with trepidation. Given the ferocity with which he expressed his opinions, I assumed he would turn out to be a crusty, tetchy bachelor. On the contrary, he was a complete charmer, the very reverse of irascible, although determined not to bend before the gales of criticism provoked by his assault on our national flower.

'I got fed up with all the troubles roses bring in their train,' he told me and my wife over tea and cake at Great Dixter. 'They get a lot of diseases and you can't replace a weak bush without changing the soil. They're quite disagreeable and make a very spotty effect even when they're flowering – a whole series of blobs.'

This was just one of the ways in which he defied horticultural correctness. He consistently advised gardeners to follow their own preferences rather than act as slaves to fashion. 'Your novice upper-class, or upper middle-class, or yuppy-class gardener will be terrified of doing the wrong thing,' he wrote in one of his *Guardian* columns, 'of growing the wrong plants, of combining them stridently and, worst of all, of being commented on adversely by "friends" and acquaintances whom they regard as important. Hence the asphyxiating boredom born of the good-taste gardener, who hasn't a fresh idea in his/her head, or any desire to develop one.'

In *The Well-Tempered Garden* he vents his disdain, too, for the tribe of gardening 'experts' – presumably unaware that, on the strength of that very book, he was soon to be counted among them.

> People tend to believe what they read. There is a certain seal of authenticity about the printed word, and anyway it is much less trouble to accept someone else's dictum than officiously go out of your way to prove each point for yourself. Authors are themselves the most shameless plagiarists, and so mistakes get quickly established as traditions, and traditions are very hard to break.

He illustrates the point with a tale about a particular clematis, described by one writer as having a delightful fragrance, then widely touted as such, when in fact it has no scent all.

Great Dixter was – and remains – a popular attraction, and some of Christo's most entertaining columns were inspired by his confrontations with visitors. In one from *In My Garden*, entitled 'Other Men's Weeds', he rails at those who complain about the apparent disorder of his unmown wild-flower meadow and at people who take it on themselves to do a bit of voluntary weeding in his beds. 'Untidiness in the garden does not matter,' he assures readers, 'as long as the owner is aware of it and does not mind it himself.'

Then there are those pernickety visitors who would like to see more labels on his plants: 'When I was on my knees weeding, during our open hours, I heard a disgruntled male voice addressing me obliquely through his companions. "If the plants were labelled we should know what we were looking at." "If I was writing labels I wouldn't be here weeding," I replied. Silence.' He goes on to discuss the pros and cons (mostly cons) of labelling, pointing out that if the plant in question happens to be some way from the path, keen gardeners will have no compunction about tramping over other delicate blooms in order to read the label.

That column ends with an account of a lively altercation with a visitor who wanted to know the exact variety of a particular unlabelled veronica. He gave her the information grudgingly, insisting first that she acquire a pencil and paper to write it down. 'How glad I was to put her to the trouble . . . It was a Bank Holiday; perhaps I wasn't in the most genial of moods.' Even the best-tempered garden might be created and nurtured by an (occasionally) ill-tempered gardener.

Of MICHAEL LEAPMAN's seventeen books, only two are about gardening: the aforementioned *One Man and His Plot* and *The Ingenious Mr Fairchild*, a biography of the eighteenth-century nurseryman who was the first to hybridize two different flowers. Both are available as e-books or print-on-demand editions from Faber Finds.

The Missing Librarian

C. J. WRIGHT

Somewhere high in the Austrian Alps there may lie the body of a librarian, for that is where Robert Proctor was last seen, at the head of the Taschach valley, on the morning of Sunday, 6 September 1903.

Proctor's final day at work at the British Museum before his intended three-week holiday in the Eastern Tyrol had been Friday, 28 August. He had been planning his expedition for some time, sending off to Innsbruck for maps of the Zillertal and Otzal Alps. The former, when it arrived, he had had cut up and mounted by a man at the museum. He had also ordered maps of the Vorarlberg at Dulau's, the international booksellers on Soho Square, but these had still not come when he called for them that Friday. Nor had the ice axe he had requested from Fulpmes in the Tyrol.

However, other last-minute tasks had kept him busy. He had brought his luggage up to Waterloo that morning and arranged for it to be sent on to Charing Cross. At lunchtime he had gone there himself to buy his ticket. He had also called at the Crédit Lyonnais and exchanged sterling for francs and Austrian crowns. Like most people before setting out on a journey he was restless. He closed his diary entry that evening with the question, 'What shall I be when I open this book again three weeks hence?'

It was probably a relief to get away, at least temporarily, from the British Museum's Department of Printed Books. He had worked there for a decade as an Assistant, but the last couple of weeks had been even more stressful than usual. His current grand project was to remove all the incunabula, those books printed before 1501, from their places scattered throughout the collections to shelves in the museum's Arch Room. There he was arranging them in what came to be known as Proctor Order, first by country, then by place of publication, then by printer, finally by size. Often these details could only be determined after minute investigation of the typefaces used.

Typography fascinated him and it was a field in which he was one of the world's leading experts. He had in 1898 published a four-volume index to the incunabula in the British Museum. The Trustees had been much impressed and had asked for a full-scale catalogue but bibliographical descriptions as such bored him. Gathering together the books was a delaying tactic, a way of keeping the Trustees happy.

Sadly, Proctor was not a man who could delegate. He would not even allow library assistants to wheel the barrows of books from the stacks to the Arch Room. Sometimes they would make off with what they saw as *their* barrows and then there would be rows. Proctor was a great man for rows and in the preceding weeks there had been some spectacular ones.

The museum photographers were his particular bugbear. They disturbed him by occupying a table by the window in the Arch Room. Three weeks earlier he had actually gone on strike for a week until the authorities had given way and agreed to move them to a space in the Iron Library. No sooner had this been settled than he had had another row, this time with W. R. Wilson, one of the Assistant Keepers and a normally genial man. It was over the removal of incunabula from the presses in the Large Room. This had been so heated that even Proctor wondered if it was the end of the British Museum for him.

In fact, at the time of his departure for the Continent, his friends were deeply concerned about his state of mind. Many years later Sydney Cockerell, subsequently Director of the Fitzwilliam Museum in Cambridge, recalled that when Proctor had called on him just before he left for his holiday, he had said to him jokingly, 'Don't fall down a crevasse.' Proctor had looked wistful, Cockerell thought, and asked 'Why not?' They might all have been even more worried had they known of a paper of instructions he was to write the day before he set out, detailing his wishes in the event that he predeceased his mother. It ended: 'My body is to be burned, and the ashes to be cast into the sea or running water.'

In addition to affairs at the museum, there were other anxieties preying on his mind. In 1897 he had moved from Wimbledon to a house he had had built at Oxshott, then a small village near Esher. It was remote enough for Conan Doyle a few years later to choose its heathland as the location for the sinister events in 'The Adventure of Wisteria Lodge'. Influenced both by William Morris's political theories and by his love of Icelandic literature, Proctor had called his new home Midgarth, a safe haven and the realm of humans in Norse cosmology. However, the house was expensive to build; and the new Guildford line, opened via Effingham in 1885, which made possible his own move, had prepared the way for rapid development which increasingly threatened his rural idyll. As a socialist, Proctor loved mankind: he was less keen on his fellow men.

More serious still were problems with his eyes. He had been seriously short-sighted all his life. At Corpus Christi, Oxford, he had hoped to cox the college eight but had had to give up the idea – he could not see where he was steering. The close work on typefaces which formed the heart of his work put a severe strain on his sight. He was now 35. He must have wondered how much longer his eyes would hold out.

Then there was his mother. Proctor was the only child of elderly parents. His father had died when the boy was 11, and he and his mother had lived together ever since. He usually took two walking holidays a year, and she almost invariably accompanied him. But it is clear from his diaries that she was finding this a strain. After all, in 1903 she was 77. That May they had been to Corsica and Florence, and it had proved too much for her. Now he was on his own. As England slipped away in the wake of the Channel ferry, it must have seemed strange to be travelling alone.

As Proctor crossed France and approached the Alps, he may have reflected on his family history in general. Despite his political beliefs, he was proud of his antecedents. The new Greek type he had devised was called Otter Greek – a reference to the family crest – and the device he had had designed by the young Gertrude Sabey for the books to be printed in this new type included his description of the animal, 'swift moving of deep-swirling rivers'. The otter device also incorporated his family arms, three black nails on a gold field. They might almost have been the instruments of his own private Passion.

Proctor was not the first member of his family to have knowledge of mountain fastnesses. Eighty years earlier his Proctor grandfather, another Robert, had been the agent for the loan floated in London in 1822 to finance Peru's War of Independence against Spain. On his return from South America, he had published an account of his travels across the Andes from Buenos Aires to Santiago and Valparaiso, and thence to Lima. In it he described the mountains, 'grand and awful' with narrow paths and precipitous abysses, and the *casuchas*, more primitive than the Alpine refuges, built to afford a little shelter to travellers. He also noted that the slopes were dotted with wooden crosses which marked the last resting places of poor wretches who had perished crossing the Cordillera.

Even discounting these family antecedents, Proctor's enthusiasm for the Alps was not unusual for the period. A taste for mountaineering had been growing in Western Europe for half a century. Clubs of German and Austrian enthusiasts had been building huts and refuges on the more popular routes and paying for them to be manned in summer. John Ball, the Irish politician and glaciologist and first President of the Alpine Club, had published a series of Alpine guides in English, and there were also the invaluable Baedekers, which Proctor certainly used. These gave details of routes, inns and even mountain guides. The recommended season for visiting the region was mid-July to mid-September, before the snows came, so Proctor was leaving his trip slightly late.

A year before, he and his mother had travelled through Switzerland to Venice and the Po valley. On their return they had made their way into the Dolomites astride the border between Italy and the South Tyrol. On 21 June they had reached St Zyprian and Weisslahnbad with its fine view of the Rosengarten, nearly 10,000 feet high and so named for the pink hue its rocks take on at sunset. All around them jagged peaks jutted out of the snow like broken bone through flesh.

The next day, setting out early in the morning and for once leaving his mother behind, Proctor made his way up to the Grasleiten hut and tried to traverse the steep snow below the towering Kesselkogel but he was frustrated by the lack of an ice axe. He then crossed the Santner pass, down to the Vajolet hut. It was an eventful few hours. Under the Rosengarten he found an icy couloir down which he thought he could descend if he kicked his heels into the snow, but he slipped on the way down and broke his stick. He then narrowly escaped being swept away by an avalanche of stones. What did overwhelm him, however, was the majesty of the scenery. 'A memorable day,' he confided to his diary.

Such memories must still have been fresh when he reached Imst in the Tyrol early in September of the following year. The Arlberg railway along the Inn valley had been opened twenty years earlier and so he was able to send his luggage on east to Steinach, which lies south of Innsbruck on the route to the Brenner pass. He then began walking up the Pitztal, one of the many valleys down which the meltwaters from the mountains and glaciers to the south flow into the River Inn.

On his way, Proctor's path would have carried him past the picturesque Stuibenbach waterfall. At the village of St Leonard, halfway up the valley, he posted the last of the daily letters he had been writing to his mother. The cart track finally petered out at Mittelberg, almost 6,000 feet above sea level, at the foot of the Mittelberg glacier, whose icefall was thought by Ball to be the grandest in the Tyrol. He made his way south-west up the Taschachtal and spent the night at the Taschach hut.

The next morning, 6 September, he set out from the refuge to make his way south-west along the edge of the Sexegerten glacier. He then had a choice of routes across the icy wilderness. He had told the attendant at the Taschach hut that he would make for the Rauhekopf hut. In this case, his path should have taken him further south-west over a spur of the Hintere Ölgrubenspitze to the head of the Kaunsertal, the next valley to the west. No one knows if he tried to take it. For Proctor the librarian was never seen again.

C. J. WRIGHT was Keeper of Manuscripts at the British Library until his retirement in 2005. Proctor's ordinary diaries, though not his official or holiday diaries, have been published in a limited edition: John Bowman (ed.), *A Critical Edition of the Private Diaries of Robert Proctor: The Life of a Librarian at the British Museum* (Lewiston, New York, and Lampeter, Wales: Edwin Mellen Press, 2010).

Coming attractions

ANDREW NIXON receives some concrete information from Jonathan Meades · HELEN MACEWAN searches for love with Charlotte Brontë · ADAM SISMAN relives the last days of Hitler · POSY FALLOWFIELD puts to sea with Richard Hughes · JUSTIN MAROZZI meets a modest mountaineer · LINDA LEATHERBARROW remembers Penelope Fitzgerald at the Highgate Library · MICHAEL HOLROYD explores the paradoxical character of Frank Harris · ANN KENNEDY SMITH takes some linguistic instruction

Bibliography